THE TE

The
Teenage Survival Kit

PETE GILBERT

KINGSWAY PUBLICATIONS
EASTBOURNE

Printed in Great Britain for
KINGSWAY PUBLICATIONS LTD
1 St. Anne's Road, Eastbourne, E. Sussex BN21 3UN by
Clays Ltd, St. Ives plc
Typeset by Nuprint Ltd, Harpenden, Herts.

Contents

This book is dedicated with my love and thanks to my mother and father, who taught me, by their love for each other and for their children, so much of what it means to be loved by God.

My thanks go to all my Christian brothers and sisters in Waltham Forest, North East London, for their patience as I learned some of the lessons in this book by practising on them! And especially to Mrs Margaret McSweeney for her willingly given painstaking help in typing this manuscript.

The Bit Everyone Skips

This is an introduction, but please don't skip this bit. After all, if you read this and decide it's no good, think of the time you'll save not wading through the rest!

Someone (not me!) could have written a whole book on each one of the subjects of the next twelve chapters. I've had to pick and choose, dip in and out of the topics. But I hope there's enough here to grab your interest. To excite you. To encourage you. I didn't write this book to fill time—I wrote it for you. And it's my earnest desire that it is helpful and practical. If it is, then praise God! If it's not, blame me!

I wrote it for Christians roughly between 15 and 19 years old. But if you're not in that category, either by age or by conviction, please read it anyway, especially if, as yet, you're not a Christian. Have a look at some of the pain, excitement, frustration, joy and challenge that could lie ahead for you. This book could do nothing better than introduce you to the best man who ever lived. He lives still.

So please read on. Learn about the kingdom. Better still, meet the King.

I

Sold Out and Filled Up

Commitment and the Holy Spirit

There was a time when World of Sport on TV on Saturdays was just football. In recent years, though, they've diversified in order to appeal to an increasingly wide range of sports spectators. That's why one Saturday afternoon recently I watched a daring, and I suppose dangerous, demonstration of a new TV sport called 'solo climbing'. Now for those of you who have never heard of solo climbing, let me explain. Apparently it's a kind of sport where the climber works his or her way up an often sheer rock face, unaided. And by unaided I don't just mean on their own. I mean without any climbing equipment even! No clamps, ropes or pitons—just hands and feet and plenty of courage!

Building on cobwebs

Watching the televised climb reminded me of a story I'd heard, alleged to be true, that took place about five years ago in the USA. The 'hero' of the story was a man called Harry. Harry was a bank clerk with a normal nine-to-five job. Harry was very ordinary, perhaps even a bit boring, but he nursed a secret ambition. He longed to be rich and famous. Living and working in a bank in New York as he did, there seemed little chance of Harry ever realizing his dreams. Then one lunchtime (the story goes) Harry is walking down the street towards a group of young lads playing baseball in the road. The pitcher made a good throw, the batsman swung and hit a great strike. The ball curved up in an arc, and landed on the roof of a nearby tenement building.

Now those older buildings full of apartments have no direct access to the roof, so the ball seemed lost. Until, that is, Harry passed by. All the lads crowded round the bank clerk until his back was to the building, and the guy with the bat stood in front of Harry. 'We want our ball back,' he demanded. Timid little Harry gulped and asked what they meant. What could he do about it? 'If you don't get the ball back for us, we'll break your legs with this bat!' This didn't seem much of a choice to Harry, who could see they meant business, and in sheer desperation he did an incredible thing. Putting down his briefcase, Harry began to climb up the outside of the building. Solo climb. No gear. Up onto the first window ledge he climbed, then scrambled up a drainpipe. Then across to the next window. And so on. Trembling like a leaf he eventually made it to the roof, drew a deep breath, found the ball, and threw it down to the street. Then he began the difficult descent, wondering all the while what the lads would do to him when he got back to ground level.

As Harry stepped onto the pavement, all the players crowded round him, and began to slap him on the back, congratulating him almost in awe. And suddenly Harry felt appreciated, a hero, someone special. This could be it! Supposing he chucked in his job at the bank, and solo climbed buildings as a stunt, all round the USA?! And that's exactly what Harry did. Over the next three years he became rich and famous as a daring stunt man, climbing public buildings for charity or publicity stunts.

Then, two years or so ago, Harry was contacted by an insurance company who were about to open the equivalent of London's National Westminster Bank building—the tallest building in their city, ninety-three floors high. 'Would Harry climb it as an opening publicity stunt?' They'd pay him twenty-five thousand dollars. This was his biggest offer yet and the highest climb. Harry phoned back the next day, and setting a date for one week's time, said yes.

A week goes by, and the day dawns at last. Harry is taken to the building by the Police, who have stopped the cars three blocks away because of the crowds. Escorted through the throng, Harry reaches the cordoned-off base of the building, finds a mass of press photographers, radio and sound engineers, and cable TV cameras. Rigged with a radio mike so the climb could be heard live, Harry begins his solo climb. Onto the first window ledge, then shins up an electrical conduit to the second window ledge. Then across the corner of the building to work up the ornamental facing stone, and all the while talking his way through the climb to millions of Americans tuned in on TV or radio. As Harry gets higher, necks are craned, binoculars abound.

After twelve hours' solid climbing, Harry at last nears the top of the building. In failing light he realizes he's made a fatal error in not first checking the building he was to climb. Just above him is a ledge, jutting two feet outwards and upwards from the building. Harry is trapped below it, ninety-three floors up, exhausted from his climb, his reputation and twenty-five thousand dollars at stake, and the light fading. Over the radio mike millions of Americans hear Harry's strained voice saying, 'I think I can make out a crack in the ledge. I'm going to straighten my legs, push off up and backwards outwards from the wall, reach with my arms, try and get my fingers in the crack, and swing my body over and onto the roof. Here goes.' Ninety-three floors up Harry pushes up, out and away. He reaches out for the crack—and plummets to the ground below.

There had to be an inquest, of course. Apparently the only thing that held his body together through the terrible G forces of the fall was the clothes he was wearing. And strangely, Harry's fists were tightly clenched. When they came to prise his fists open, they found across the palm of one hand…a cobweb. When they played back the video and radio tape, they reckoned Harry had mistaken the cobweb for a crack in the fading light. He trusted his life to an illusion, a mistake, a cobweb. It had, of course, let him down. And the disappointment had proved fatal.

Forgive the length at which I've told that story. It's just that it seems to describe what so many of us do. We base our lives on illusion instead of on reality. We live for the next experience (be it a video, disco, girlfriend, money, sex) instead of for God. And it doesn't work. And you end up getting hurt.

Let me ask a simple question. Consider your experience of Christianity right now. Consider this God we talk about, and this man Jesus Christ and his Holy Spirit. How does your experience match up to the claims and promises of the Bible? Think about it. Close your eyes if it helps. Have you experienced the reality of the promises we find in the Bible: 'I have come that they may have life, and have it to the full' (John 10:10) or, 'The Father will give you whatever you ask in my name' (John 15:16) or, 'God is faithful; he will not let you be tempted beyond what you can bear' (1 Corinthians 10:13)? Or have you only read these words and never really experienced them? It took me seven years as a Christian to realize that if the Bible says something in black and white, then it means exactly what it says, and is totally trustworthy. Even on the many occasions that I've failed God, he has *never* let me down. So if my experience is different from what God promises in his word, who is wrong? I've discovered it's *always* me.

Real or fake?

Now that's hard to swallow. It hurts our pride. It's mind boggling, but it's true. And honesty about yourself before God is where commitment to him really starts. God can accept, understand, forgive and change the very worst about us. It's only when we pretend that he can't do anything.

We must ask ourselves a question and answer honestly: does our Christian life work or not? God is very practical and he made us practical too. Either Christianity works, or it doesn't. Either God is at fault, or we are. It's just like the poster says, 'If God seems far away, guess who moved.' If in all honesty you know your Christian experience is sadly lacking in reality, let me suggest why that may be so. It's often because Jesus Christ didn't come simply to be your Saviour. In the New Testament that phrase is used far fewer times than the phrase 'Jesus is Lord'. For every time that Jesus is called Saviour, he is called Lord nine times. If Jesus is just your Saviour, you've only got half a gospel. This man is King Jesus. Nothing less. So if he lives in you only to forgive your sins and not to run your life, then I promise you your Christianity won't work.

Christianity only works when Jesus is both Saviour and Lord in your life day by day. If you consciously give Jesus less than one hundred per cent, then you'll be powerless, apathetic and miserable. You'll have enough of Jesus to spoil the enjoyment of your sins, because you'll know they're wrong and hurt God, others and you. But you'll have enough of sin to spoil your relationship with God, because you'll feel a hypocrite in your youth group, and church. And so you end up with one foot in either camp, torn in two and miserable in both. You are a fifty-fifty Christian.

Is *this* your reality? Is this the Christian illusion that you're living out, varying from apathy, through faked spirituality, to despair? Have you grabbed at a cobweb only to find it doesn't hold you? If so, what can you do about it? The starting point is to be honest. Be honest before God.

All or nothing

What next? The second step is commitment. That's a very unpopular word these days. The old cults of the seventies (the Moonies, the Jonestown Group, etc.), which required absolute blind obedience, have passed away and been replaced by a kind of easy-come easy-go drifting into pseudo-scientific philosophies that demand little or no commitment. Youth marriages, one-parent families, divorces, abortions abound and are in some degree due to *lack of commitment* to God's laws and to other people. So commitment is generally an old-fashioned and little liked or even understood word.

But commitment is your next step if you want to break the vicious circle of unreality and hypocrisy in your Christian life. How does it work?

Well, once you've been honest about where you're actually at with God, you have to be honest about where you want to be. God knows where he wants you, what he wants to change in you, and do through you. He is King, and it's his prerogative to direct your life. But it's your God-given privilege to say 'no'. At the end of the day people are as holy as they *want* to be. God sets no limit on how near he'll draw to you or how much he'll use you for good. We are the ones who set the limits.

Commitment is closely connected with the kingship of Jesus Christ. It works by letting the Holy Spirit search your heart and bring to the surface those hidden things, secret desires and concealed sins, which hinder your walk with Jesus. Commitment to the kingship of Jesus gives him the absolute right to your obedience whether you understand, want it or like it. So when God shows you areas of your life that aren't yet under the rule of King Jesus, commitment works by causing you to make a decision. You have to make a choice. You either choose to change and bring that matter under the kingship of Jesus, or you choose to keep God out and experience guilt, frustration, confusion and lack of power. Make no mistake, no one drifts by accident into sin. We choose the direction; God's or ours. The choices come daily and the need for commitment never ends.

Let me give you two examples from the Bible. In John 20 Jesus Christ appears to the disciples after his resurrection. They're delighted, but Thomas the twin is missing. I can't help wondering where was Thomas? It's clear he hadn't just popped out to the loo or down to the local! The disciples were petrified and had locked themselves into the upper room. My feeling is that Thomas was on the fringe of things. You know the type, a regular attender, one of the gang, but not fully involved. Reserving the right to be an individual, to opt out if he wants to. Consequently Thomas misses out on seeing Jesus. When the disciples tell Thomas about Jesus' resurrection, he doesn't believe them. Now I can't blame Thomas too much for that. The disciples had to see Jesus before they believed and understood. And Jesus himself accommodated Thomas' request and showed him the wounds. I don't think the problem was that Thomas doubted. He hadn't seen Jesus like the others had. He didn't have our advantage of two thousand years of changed lives and answered prayers to back up the claim of a *living* Jesus. I think the problem was that Thomas doubted because *he hadn't been there*. He may well have lacked that wholehearted commitment to God and to his people. But look what happens. Faced with the living Jesus, Thomas falls down and says, 'My Lord and my God'. Two separate titles. He wasn't repeating himself. He recognized Jesus as God and he claimed him as Lord. Boss. The King. Commitment based on honesty will lead you to the kingship of Jesus.

King Jesus

The kingship of Jesus will require two things of you. First, you are required to obey and second, you must repent when you fail to obey. Repentance grows out of commitment and it challenges the reality of your Christian life. What do you do when you've done/thought/said something wrong? Shrug it off? Try harder next time? Try to push it under the carpet and carry on sinning? Or are you honest enough to say, 'This is wrong. It hurts a holy God. It'll hurt others and it'll hurt me.' Then you are faced with a decision, 'I'll carry on sinning,' or, 'I'll stop.' Note, not: 'I want to stop, but....' Repentance is an act of your will, when you declare to God, 'I *will* stop.' It means you've decided to say 'No' before you next get into an area of temptation.

Repentance and commitment to Jesus mean you have to act on your decision. The Bible tells us to flee temptation, which means move away from, avoid it. So you avoid the disco if there you are tempted to drink too much, or slow-dance in a sexually provocative way. You avoid the top shelf of the local newsagents. It may mean, as one of my friends recently discovered, the destruction of posters, books, records, clothes, or jewellery. Some of those things weren't bad in themselves, but they were born out of my friend's deliberate choice to ignore God and rebel at one stage of his Christian life. So they had to go.

Our God is a holy and a jealous God. If you're not prepared to go to any lengths for him, then you must seriously and honestly question your commitment to him. The pressures on young people are such that God demands and is proud of radical sons and daughters. A good maxim is 'if in doubt, cut it out!' If it is doubtful (be it your girlfriend, your fashion, your social life), then stop, say sorry, decide to change, and move in the opposite direction because it's not worth risking your walk with Jesus over anything.

David had to learn this lesson in a very painful way. In this second example in 2 Samuel 11–12 David chose deliberately to covet, to commit adultery, and then to murder. Sin always leads you deeper into sin, guilt and pain. He was eventually confronted by the word of God through a prophet, and chose to repent. This David was a man anointed with power by God. He was a man after God's heart and an ancestor of Jesus himself. David realized, following the confrontation with Nathan the prophet of God, that he had sinned 'against thee only, O God' (Psalm 51:4). This does not mean that David could ignore what he had done to Uriah or Bathsheba. Indeed he couldn't ignore it, because although he was for- given by God, David had to endure the results of his sin, as his illegitimate child later died. And later on still, his son Absalom rebelled against him. No, David realized that God is King and he sets the rules, and David broke them, so it was to God that David was primarily responsible.

Commitment shows you that sin goes against the face of God. For us the confrontation usually comes from the living word of God made flesh, Jesus Christ himself, not via a prophet and the spoken word of God. And commitment that leads to repentance can be painful and costly. But you can be sure that the cost of disobedience is far greater than the cost of obedience. I suggest you read that last sentence again—I think it's worth living by.

Gritted teeth or walk by the Spirit

That leads me on to the third key factor when we're looking at this issue of the King of kings. If the first is honest reality, the second repentant commitment, then the third is a person, the Holy Spirit. I am not advocating that we all grit our teeth and try harder to be a 'better person'. You know that doesn't work. How many times have you been honest with yourself, seen sin in your life, confessed it and then determined to change? Commitment isn't something you can simply decide to do. Oh yes, God looks for your co-operation. But it's not just a matter of your resolving to do more, be better, or go to more meetings. So what else is there?

Galatians 3:1-3 puts it in a nutshell. Paul is writing to a church that has been going on O.K., but is in danger of being swamped by people who insist that the way into the kingdom of God is through self effort, outward appearances and trying harder to earn the salvation of God. Paul calls them foolish! Idiots! The reason is that they became Christians by believing in Jesus (by faith) whereupon they received the Holy Spirit as a gift. In Galatians Paul exhorts people to continue as they have begun *through the Holy Spirit*, and not through their own efforts.

No power, no sale!

Last January I was trying to sell my car. For two years my H Registration Mark 2 Cortina had served me faithfully, but after the replacement engine eventually seized up, it became obvious I needed a more reliable vehicle. So I decided to put the car in the local paper for sale for a nominal sum. One dark, rainy night in January there was a ring at the front door, and there were two men who wanted to look the car over. Eager to sell, I grabbed a torch and the car keys, and we began the transaction. After inspecting the inside, outside and underside of the car and looking under the bonnet, the two men asked if they could drive the car round the block. No trouble, I said, and tried to start the engine. There were a couple of sick-sounding engine whirrs, then nothing! You can imagine the scene. I grinned redly at the two guys and said, 'She's just cold! I'll adjust the choke, and you'll see, she'll start right away!' So I fiddled with the choke, pumped the accelerator and generally tried to look as though I knew what I was doing. Then (as a last resort!) I prayed a bit and turned the ignition key. Click. Nothing else! Eventually I had to admit defeat. And guess what? I didn't sell the car to those two guys. In fact, it eventually went for scrap at £25. No power…no sale.

I've found the same principle is equally true for my Christian life, and it might be true for yours too. If you desire to be one hundred per cent committed to Jesus, then the Holy Spirit is the only one who can so change you and empower you from the inside that the commitment sticks. And better yet, it becomes a pure delight! No power…no sale. No Holy Spirit…no lasting commitment and no real working Christianity.

There are a number of different words used in the Bible for the Holy Spirit. In the Old Testament one of the main words used is the Hebrew *ruach*, which carries with it the idea of a rushing, sweeping, cleansing wind; unseen, blowing wherever it wants to. This word conveys a sense of the majesty and might of God. The winds which swept over the desert are the same winds that the eagles ride, taking the air currents over the storms, wings locked, flying into the sun with eyes shielded by a special membrane. The Holy Spirit is given to you to enable you to ride over the storms of life, the hassles and disappointments. You lock your own wings, that's your commitment to fly with God, but it's the wind of his Holy Spirit that carries you. And you fly straight for the face of Jesus Christ the Son of God himself.

In the New Testament the word most commonly used for the Spirit is the Greek word *pneuma*. It's the root for our word 'pneumatic', and the sense of the word is similar. The Holy Spirit is the one who fills us out to the shape we were meant to be, who firms us up on the inside, so we don't change shape (our behaviour) when there's outside pressure, like a balloon would when squeezed.

There's a third word linked to the Holy Spirit in the new Testament, and that's the Greek word for power, *dunamis*, from which we get the word 'dynamite'. Now take these three different facets of the Holy Spirit, the cleansing, lifting, infilling shaping power of God. That's what I need to make my commitment work. I build the mould, but God fills it with his Holy Spirit. My co-operation, his life; my availability, his ability. So how does it work?

Through jargon to experience

There's a lot of controversy about the Holy Spirit. I'd like to cut through it by looking simply to the Bible. Every Christian has received the Holy Spirit. You can only be born into the kingdom of God by the Holy Spirit (John 3:5; Romans 8, 9, 16). The Holy Spirit has been given to each Christian as a seal or guarantee that we no longer belong to ourselves, but to God, who bought us at a price, and guarantees our status in his kingdom, and our future (Ephesians 1:13–14). That guarantee was finally obtained as Jesus cried in triumph from the cross, 'It is finished.' It's the same phrase that was stamped across bills that were settled, and it means 'paid in full'. The guarantee provided by the Holy Spirit is yours because the bill for your sins has been paid by Jesus Christ. So as a Christian you are born and sealed by the Holy Spirit.

Yet there's a third emphasis in Scripture that can be traced right through from the Old Testament (Joel 2:28–29) to the New Testament (John 1:33; Acts 1:5; Ephesians 5: 18): 'Be filled with the Spirit.' It's a command, so obviously it's possible to receive the Spirit and yet not to be filled or baptized (i.e. saturated) with his power. It's a bit like keeping water behind a dam, instead of releasing it.

On holiday in Scotland a couple of years ago I visited a hydroelectric power station built at the foot of a gorge inside a mountain called Ben Cruachan. The idea was that water pumped up the mountainside during cheap offpeak electricity hours at night was released from the dam at peak time during the day and would drive generators to provide power. Without the release there was no power.

I spent seven years of my Christian life really believing all the right things, even saying and doing some of the right things, but without that one hundred per cent commitment or the Holy Spirit power to see it begin to be fulfilled. My church background argued against any 'experience' of God through the Holy Spirit after conversion. Spiritual gifts were really only natural gifts given over to God's service. I was only shaken out of this half-and-half world by meeting Christians at college who were radically different from me, who showed real love and determination, who talked of God as though they knew him and his personality. Their lifestyle convinced me I was missing out. They put the spotlight on my Christian hypocrisy, and made me begin to look at myself in honest reality for the first time. Then came that moment when I wanted to give one hundred per cent commitment, when I took everything I had, good and bad, and gave it to God, saying, 'O.K., if you can use even me as I now see myself to be, then do it. I'm yours.' And he did. In my room in college, on my own, I cried and cried, and God filled me with his Holy Spirit. The release of his power had begun.

The present continuous

I'm constantly being shown areas of my life that lack that commitment to the lordship of Christ. Ephesians 5:18 makes it clear that's only the beginning. The precise Greek means 'go on being filled'. It's called a present continuous tense! That's why the early church picked 'men known to be full of the Spirit and wisdom' (Acts 6:3). Note it doesn't say 'men who have *been filled* in the past'. I'm still convinced it was never meant to be a second experience, but an ongoing part of radical conversion. (If you want to look into this further, see the message that Peter preached in Acts 2:1–7 and the way the disciples in Acts 19:1–7 are presented as an unusual exception.) It's *not* a matter of first- and second-class Christians; it was never meant to be optional to be filled with Holy

Spirit power, but vital to realistic practical Christian living.

Why is it so vital? How does the Holy Spirit complete the chain of honest reality and commitment? He's rather like a prism. He reflects everything of God that you and I know. Or like a filter, the Holy Spirit shows us truth, and is the channel for all of our growth in Jesus. You read your Bible through the aid of the Holy Spirit (1 Corinthians 2:9–16), just as it was written with the aid of the Holy Spirit (2 Timothy 3:16; John 16:13). You pray with the help of the Holy Spirit (Romans 8:26–27). You witness with the assistance of the Holy Spirit (Acts 1:8). And so it is throughout the whole of your Christian life. So you need as much of the power and person of the Holy Spirit as possible! I'm not arguing for a theology based on experience alone, but neither should we accept a theology based on lack of experience. The New Testament was written to explain truth already experienced, not what should happen theoretically!

It's the job of the Holy Spirit to convince you on the inside concerning sin (John 16:9–11). The more you go on in God, the more aware you become of your sin. That's counterbalanced by seeing more of the righteousness of God and his desire and ability to forgive. It's the Holy Spirit who convicts you concerning the victory of Jesus Christ over death, sin and Satan, and of the plight and destination of those who reject Jesus.

Fruits and gifts

The Holy Spirit also builds into your life the fruit of the character of God. As you're changed inside, so the evidence of the Holy Spirit becomes clearer through the nature of the fruit that your character bears. It's simple really—you're just being changed 'from glory into glory' to become more like Jesus, while retaining the uniqueness that he first created in your personality. The fruit of the Holy Spirit has nine aspects, and we are meant to have them all: love, joy, peace, patience, kindness, goodness, faithfulness, gentleness, self-control (Galatians 5:22). Try that list against your own life (be honest!) and you'll soon see that we all need everything of God we can have!

The gifts of the Holy Spirit are mentioned as operating throughout the Old Testament and New Testament, but are most clearly listed in 1 Corinthians 12 and Romans 12. It's not a complete list, but we'll look at them here briefly.

The message of wisdom: You can see an example of this in John 8:7. In difficult, tense or confused situations a word of wisdom brings clarity, challenge, understanding and a potential for God's solution of the problem. A phrase or statement beyond the ability or natural wisdom of the speaker is marked by love and peace in the giver.

The message of knowledge: A good example can be found in Jesus' remarks in John 4:18. This knowledge came by supernatural revelation from God. Jesus couldn't have known the marriage situation of the woman at the well at Sychar unless he was told directly by God through the Holy Spirit. (Remember that, although Jesus was God, he carried out his earthly ministry as a man in the power of the Holy Spirit.) A word of knowledge isn't 'mental telepathy' or 'spiritual snooping'. It's given by God so that you can be involved in serving and helping, but not so that you can be one-up over the other bloke! Words of knowledge are particularly useful in counselling situations when the real problem isn't emerging. Or in healing, when God identifies an individual by revealing through the Holy Spirit what the symptoms are to someone who can then pray for that healing. Or in prayer, when the Holy Spirit reveals the person or circumstance he wants praying over.

Faith: The gift of the Holy Spirit that goes beyond the faith exercised in conversion. This gift is a specific exercising of faith for a particular project ahead. It's the kind of faith in God that gives martyrs their strength or enabled George Müller to believe God for the millions of pounds used for the setting up of his Training College and Homes for Children in

the face of enormous opposition. It's a gift needed to spear-
head great ventures for God that on the face of them seemed
impossible. Hebrews 11 gives some biblical examples of this
gift of faith.

Gifts of healing: These are exercised where physical,
emotional, mental and spiritual healing are needed. Jesus
suffered beating and scourging, not because of the will of a
sadistic or vindictive God. The cross bought you the potential
for spiritual healing and wholeness; the whipping post bought
you the potential for physical and emotional healing (Isaiah
53:5).

Miraculous powers: It might be thought that all the supernatural gifts of the Holy Spirit are miraculous, being endowed
by God and suspending his natural laws, but the Bible uses the
term 'miraculous powers' to describe a particular category of
events not covered by the other gifts. Jesus demonstrated this
on a number of occasions by turning water into wine (John
2:1–11); feeding 5,000 people with five loaves and two fishes
(John 6:1–14); or raising the dead (John 11:38–47).

Prophecy: This gift of the Spirit is for the comfort, encouraging,
or exhorting of the church. It need not foretell the future, and
is rarely directional (i.e., 'the Lord says to you, John Smith,
go to the African Jungle!'). Prophecy will often come as a seal
or a focus to something you have already been hearing or
been seeking from the Lord. In keeping with Jewish (Old
Testament) traditions of passing on verbal messages,
prophecy should really be given in the first person (i.e., 'I am
your God who has forgiven you,' and not, 'The Lord says
that it is your God who has forgiven you'), although it should
be remembered that any prophecy will contain a certain
percentage of the giver rather than God, and to that extent
will rarely be totally accurate. It's never, for example, on a
par with the Bible. Nor will it ever contradict Scripture,
which is the foundation or springboard for all thought and
revelation from your living God.

When the Holy Spirit's gift of prophecy is the major feature of a person's service under God (their ministry) then such a person will be a prophet. Prophetic ministry is affirmed by the gifting of Jesus himself (Eph 4:7–12) and is foundational to the building of his church. Because a prophet's main function will be to prophesy, he is likely to be more accurately portraying God's heart and mind, than if he were occasionally using the gift of the Spirit as you or I might. In other words, the *ministry* of a prophet (from Jesus) will be exercised more frequently with greater accuracy by a prophet, than will the *gift* of prophecy (from the Holy Spirit) by people like you and me. So expect God to speak, but do test all prophecy, by Scripture, by the Holy Spirit inside you, by circumstances, and by those you respect in the Lord. A prophet is never out of control when prophesying as 'the Spirit of the prophet is subject to the prophet' (1 Corinthians 14:32). Jesus himself exercised this gift of prophecy in Matthew 24:51.

Distinguishing between spirits: this is often called the gift of discernment. It is the ability from God to recognize what spiritual forces you are up against in a situation or person. Again this is a useful gift in counselling, and is a vital 'homing device' when targeting your prayers more selectively against the enemy. Discernment often reveals a whole dimensional reality as to why people say and do the things they do. It distinguishes the supernaturally good from the supernaturally bad. It is useful in checking the other spiritual gifts too.

Different kinds of tongues: This is the only gift in the list which can be used for private benefit as well as the building of the church. James 3 tells of the potency of the tongue for good or evil. Speaking in tongues (languages) is the direct communication of your spirit with God's Holy Spirit, bypassing your conscious (but not necessarily your sub-conscious) thoughts and your mental barriers. None of the gifts of the Holy Spirit cause you to lose control, as God's Holy Spirit is a spirit of self-control and discipline (2 Timothy 1:7). Some of them are power gifts where we are merely a channel (e.g., healing, miracles) whereas others depend more on our initiative in reaching out to God. Tongues (as well as prophecy and interpretation) lie in this area. The gift is used either in private prayer to ease worship (when you've run out of superlatives to tell God how great he is!), or in intercession (when you don't know how or what to pray), or it can be used publicly, in which case it must be exercised with order and with an interpretation. This message in tongues can be either from you Godward, or from God to you. The tongue or language can be either a human language or an 'angelic' language. The most dramatic example of the gift is found in Acts 2:1–13.

The interpretation of tongues: Please note, this gift is the interpretation, but not the translation, of tongues! When a public message in another language is given, it should be followed by an interpretation, a gift whereby God reveals the emphasis of the message for the people. It's unlikely to be a word-for-word translation! Like any language, repeated phrases and vocal inflections can often be highlighted in the interpretation as well as in the original message, and you can often pick these out when listening to the language and its interpretation.

The other gifts in Romans 12 are self-explanatory, so I won't insult your intelligence by outlining them! It may well be that as you read this book you are already familiar with the gifts and their functions, or that you are actually using them, in which case please forgive the lengths at which I've simply explained the gifts. If there are areas you are unfamiliar with, then I hope I've whetted your appetite to press on into God for everything he has for you, in Jesus, through the Holy Spirit. Either way, read on, because I want now to be very practical about the Holy Spirit and his gifts.

It's for you!

There are only a few reasons why you might not have experienced the reality of God's kingdom through the gifts of his Holy Spirit. The first may well be wrong teaching. Some maintain that the gifts were for the early church only and have now ceased to be. I reckon that if the Apostles needed the gifts then I most certainly do! (and so do you!). The verses used in this argument are usually 1 Corinthians 13:8–10, which some argue refers to the perfection of Scripture. It is argued that when the Scripture is complete and Jesus Christ's work is done, the gifts will disappear. But perfection in this passage refers to Jesus and his second coming; we don't yet see 'face to face' (verse 12). The gifts (promised from the Old Testament onwards) are for now. They're for you. That's why Peter said in Acts 2:38–39 that the promise is for all. That's why Jesus in Matthew 28:20 commanded his disciples to teach everything he had commanded them, and that includes healing the sick, casting out demons, etc. Jesus even gives us the additional startling promise that his disciples would do 'greater works than these' (John 14:12).

The second very common reason that blocks people's experience of the Holy Spirit is fear. Many people, perhaps particularly girls, are scared that God will 'take them over' and make them do something ridiculous. So they remain frozen, desperately wanting more of God, but scared to reach out, ask, experience. But the Holy Spirit is a perfect gentleman and knows exactly what we need and what our personality is like. So for some the filling of the Holy Spirit will be dramatic—some people are so relaxed they just rest in the Holy Spirit, even gently falling over as the Holy Spirit does a deep work in their lives. (This is quite biblical; Adam, Abraham, Elijah, John and many more had a deep experience of God during supernaturally induced sleep, or fell to the ground in encounters with him.) Others may cry, laugh or feel peaceful. Others still may tremble, or feel warm, or cool. There's no set pattern. And there's nothing to fear. God often does give immediate gifts, and the most common is speaking in tongues, but that's not necessarily so, and isn't biblically the 'first evidence' of baptism by the Holy Spirit. It's simply that as a basic gift it's one of the earliest of God's gifts. There's nothing wrong in natural human caution, but fear that binds isn't of God, and his love can get rid of it (Luke 11:13; 1 John 4:18).

The final main reason that prevents God from giving to us what he longs to through the gifts of his Holy Spirit is sin. There's a spiritual principle that you can see time and again in the lives of Bible characters, and that is that God cannot raise that which has not died (John 12:24–26). It's futile to ask God to fill you with his Holy Spirit and yet deliberately and wilfully to continue to sin in areas in your life. God won't pour his pure Holy Spirit into deliberately soiled buckets! Day-by-day living sacrifice, honest repentance and commitment are prerequisites to going on being filled with the Holy Spirit. I don't mean we have to be perfect before God can fill us, but we do have to want with all our hearts to be like Jesus and have his attitude to our sins before God is able to give us the power to dislodge some of them. But equally, some sins won't be dislodged *until* we've been filled.

What if you really want to be filled? You have been honest in offering one hundred per cent commitment to Jesus and have overcome the tugs of fear. What next? I advise you to find someone you can trust to pray with. Someone of the same sex as yourself, older in Jesus than you are, who is filled with the Holy Spirit. Not a crank, or a rebel from a split church, but some mature Christian, preferably from your own church, who will want to pray with you, and probably lay hands on you! Now that's nothing magical, but it is the New Testament symbol of God using your brothers and sisters in Jesus to pass on his power to you (Acts 7:6; 1 Tim 1:6). As they pray for you, you *receive* in faith. Don't pray at the same time, or nobody does the receiving!

Developing your spiritual muscles

After that it's partly up to you. Like muscles, spiritual gifts have to be used in order to develop. That means that within a few days of being first filled with the Holy Spirit you'll experience 'spiritual hunches'. Confronted with a person or situation you will suddenly feel quite clearly what the real underlying issues are. Or you will say exactly the right thing at the right time. Or God may give you a picture in your mind that he wants you to deliver prophetically. Then you'll doubt that it is God. You'll either think it's you or Satan. Now listen: Satan does counterfeit gifts, but not in a child of God who wants God's best. And if you doubt it's God, that's often a good sign that it is God. Satan would not bother assailing you with doubts otherwise! I usually do a simple check by saying to God: 'Father, if this thought (or whatever) is of you, then increase it. If it's not, then let it fade away.' Then I wait a while. Simple, but it works! But you'll need to put yourself out on a limb for God. Too many Christians live safely within the boundaries of what they can manage or cope with for themselves, and consequently never get the chance to see God at work to do the impossible.

So that's it! Sorry it took so long, but I think you'll agree it's an important subject. Honest reality. Commitment. The Holy Spirit. It's really where it all begins. And whatever lies ahead from here is going to be very exciting.

2

God's Word Works!

Bible Reading

There seem to be two automatic assumptions made about any person who becomes a Christian. One is that he or she can then pray. The other is that he or she can then read the Bible. Both assumptions are wrong. I've never met a single Christian (and that includes me) who hasn't experienced problems with these two basic areas of Christian activity. In this chapter we're going to look at how to read and study the Bible and to meditate on it, and I think we should start by debunking those two common assumptions. If we honestly admit that reading the Bible *can* be difficult, even boring, we remove a lot of the pressure and enable the unspoken difficulties to be brought into the open so that we can learn from each other's mistakes.

Only seventeen per cent of teenagers read as a pastime, so a faith which relies heavily on the written word can't be an easy matter for most of us! Don't feel you're a failure if you're going through a time when the Bible seems unapproachable to you. Join the club! But instead of being paralysed with guilt, let's look at why we should read the Bible and then how.

Why should I?

Ever since I became a Christian it's been instilled into me, without explanation, that it was necessary to read your Bible every day. It's a kind of unwritten rule, an eleventh commandment. 'Thou shalt have a quiet time every morning.' If you read your Bible out of a sense of duty, then I guarantee it will soon become a chore, stripped of relevance or enjoyment. On the other hand, if you see the reason for reading the Bible you are more likely to find it useful instead of a bind. So what *is* the reason? If it's right to read it regularly, then why?

Think about the Bible itself. It's an incredible book. Actually it's sixty-six books altogether, twenty-seven in the New Testament and thirty-nine in the Old Testament. The Bible was written over a period of some 4000 years, including 400 years between the end of the Old Testament and the beginning of the New Testament, when God's revelation to his people Israel virtually ceased! The documents contained in the New Testament were completed within approximately seventy years of the events they depict, and many of the original documents date back to the time of writing—they're not copies. In the 20,000 documents that go to make up the New Testament in its entirety there are only minor discrepancies, mostly grammatical, between accounts. Compare this with the mere 200 documents, many contradictory, which make up the historical record of the Gallic conquests of Julius Caesar in his diary! God's diary is better!

Even without checking this extraordinary book with outside references like archaeology and history (which back up its reliability), there are some remarkable factors to be considered.

Whose story?

Despite its many different authors, the same strands run throughout the weave of the Bible story. God himself intervenes in what has cornily but accurately been called 'his story'. Images used in the Old Testament are mirrored by realities in the New Testament, so that the sacrifice of a lamb to ensure the safety of the Israelites in Exodus 12 becomes the sacrifice of the Lamb of God, Jesus Christ himself, to ensure the salvation of God's people in the New Testament. These themes, or 'types', occur time and again. There are 330 prophecies in the Old Testament concerning the coming Messiah and they are all fulfilled in Jesus Christ in the New Testament. All 330 of them! The chances of even eight being fulfilled are 1:100,000,000,000,000,000. So there's something *very* special going on in this book!

At what cost?

If that doesn't stimulate you to want to look into this incredible book, then think about why it was written down so accurately by scribes from the Jewish oral tradition of exact storytelling, and preserved so incredibly for us. Think about the struggles in this country's history to earn the right for ordinary people to read the Bible in their own language. Why has there been this constant manoeuvring on God's part to preserve and spread the written record of his dealings with people? Because there is recorded within the Bible much of the character, the desires, the will and the emotions of God. The Bible reveals to us the nature of man—it's like a mirror held up to the reader. Reading this book may threaten your lifestyle! The Bible combines these two elements: God's heart and man's nature, spanned not by the written word, but the living word made flesh (John 1:14).

For what purpose?

So the ultimate answer to the question, 'Why read the Bible?' is that it reveals to you more of Jesus. The Bible is real spiritual food. By reading it regularly you grow in maturity and understanding and wisdom. You see and feel more of Jesus Christ, who is your Lord and Friend, your boss and your brother.

There are other reasons for reading the Bible too. It contains many promises from God which we need to claim, some daily (for example, 1 Corinthians 10:13). It also contains warnings from God and clear instructions for my lifestyle. I can't hope to run my life properly if I ignore the instruction manual—it's like trying to wire a plug on your stereo without taking the colour coded wires into account. And there's the vital area of faith. My level of faith will vary according to the difficulty of the circumstances around me! If things are going well, I've lots of faith. If things get rough, my faith level takes a dip. Now Romans 10 says that faith is by hearing the word of Christ, so reading the Bible builds your faith. Ask the Holy Spirit to do that for you as you read it! If you're not sleeping too well, mark as many references in the Bible on sleep as you can find (use a concordance), then read them two to three times a day to build faith in God that you can sleep peacefully in God's care. It works! The word of God is described in Proverbs 1–3 as a medicine for us, and we need to take it! If you're ill and don't have the faith to believe that Jesus wants to and can heal you, then mark the verses on healing in the Old and New Testament. Read them daily, asking the Holy Spirit to reveal them to you personally. Believing it's true because it's in the Bible is not enough. You need a personal revelation that drops the belief from your head (where you know it) to your heart (where you feel it). It's that vital eighteen inch head-heart drop! As your faith is built through the word of Christ, think what effect that will have on your prayer life.

A means to an end

Having a daily quiet time isn't an end in itself; it's a means to an end. The end is that we see more of Jesus Christ and become more like him. If it's not working—and by that I mean if it's not feeding you spiritually, showing you more of Jesus, making holiness an exciting prospect—then all you need to do is adjust your methods.

And now for the first time revealed in print is *the* secret behind the Christian quiet time. Mysteries made clear. Methods laid bare. And the secret is…there isn't one!!

There is no one correct method that will guarantee you one hundred per cent success in your quiet time. There are as many successful ways of reading the Bible as there are

Christians. All you have to do is work out what's right for *you*. Let me make a few suggestions.

...the when

Lots of Christians ask me if it's best to read the Bible first thing in the morning (the standard quiet time!) or last thing at night. Can I make two simple points? First, why be an either/or Christian, seeking the minimum requirement from God, and then grudgingly giving it? Why not be a both/and Christian, going for the maximum that God has for you, and then doing it happily in the knowledge that it's going to be and feel good for you because your heavenly Father loves you and is kind. In other words, it's very beneficial to start the day by reading the Bible; it can help to set you up for the whole day. At the same time, it's very helpful to end the day, just before going to sleep, by reading God's word. So why not do both?

The second point. If you read the Bible morning and evening, that still leaves approximately fifteen hours during the day when you might get the odd five minutes to browse a bit in the Bible, if you're carrying the New Testament around with you in your jacket. The Bible Society has just brought out a real pocket-sized full Bible, which I heartily recommend you carry.

Reading your Bible first thing in the morning is a great way to start the day, and God will often use the reading during events of that day. If you're anything like me first thing in the morning, it's difficult to wake up and concentrate, but there are ways around that. Set your alarm ten minutes before you need to be alert, and gradually 'soak' out of sleep! Keep your Bible near your bed so that it is easily within reach. Keep a bookmark at the place you're reading. If you're really bad at getting up, keep your Bible next to the alarm clock—on the other side of the room! You see, there are always ways and means, it's just a matter of adjustment. But it's like slimming—no matter how many aids and methods you have, if you don't want to lose weight enough, you won't. It's the same with reading the Bible. Personally, I read it first thing and last thing each day. That's not heroic, but it is useful.

...the where

The next most common question is: 'Where do I read the Bible?' Well, if you're very tired first thing or last thing, then reading in bed will probably be disastrous. It's certainly more effective than Horlicks! I'm used to doing a lot of reading (I 'did' English Literature at College) so I don't find that a problem. But if you find yourself nodding off, then adjust! Get up and wash first. Or read standing up. Or even standing on your head! Anything that works for you. In summer it might be good to read outside in the garden. Here in London lots of folks read as they commute on trains, the tube or buses. I think reading where there are others around is fine as an extra, but I do think it is important that you spend some time reading alone, where it's quiet. Although most quiet times would be better for being noisier! But we'll touch on that in a later chapter about worship, praise and prayer.

....and the how

The first point I'd make is discipline. It takes approximately three weeks to form a habit, so if you stick at reading regularly for that length of time, then you'll probably form a habit which will help on the discipline side. This is a good reason for keeping to a regular time of reading, as consistency makes for a more quickly established habit.

The second point is that quality comes before quantity. I know Christians who, in their keenness to get into the Bible, have 'burned themselves out' by trying to read too much too soon. It is sometimes necessary to have a one-and-a-half hour's quiet time, but it's difficult to keep that up day in day out. Much better to keep to something you can manage, which is actually feeding you spiritually on a *daily* basis. So

I'd rather do a regular twenty minutes a day of Bible reading and prayer than one-and-a-half hours a day for only four days. Eating less and regularly is better for you than stuffing your face and then fasting. So too with Bible reading.

Help along the way

What about using Bible reading aids? There are so many notes available nowadays that the problem is deciding which. Again, find the ones that suit you. I don't use Bible reading notes regularly, preferring to choose my own Bible reading, but I do use them when discipline slips, because then at least I have a regular pattern to help me get back into the habit. As long as you avoid the danger of ending up reading the notes instead of your Bible, Bible notes can be very helpful. The best that I've come across are *AM/PM* and *Jam* by Scripture Union, or *Every Day with Jesus* by Crusade for World Revival, if you're a bit more used to reading. Bible notes that demand committing a verse to memory or ask questions of their readers and suggest activities are the best.

You'll have noticed that it's not only the notes that come in every shape and size, but the Bible itself is available in so many different versions. Again the important thing is to find one which you get on with. My own feeling is that for study purposes the best version is the New American Standard, because I think it's the most careful translation, if you can ignore the American spelling. But if I want a good read of the Bible I use the New International Version, or the Good News Bible. Funnily enough, perhaps because of my upbringing, I tend to have memorized verses mainly from the Authorized Version, but it really is a bit too old-fashioned for my every-day use.

Are you one of those people who have a horror of writing in books? I used to think it was sacrilege to write in a Bible, but it's really very practical. I try to mark things in my Bible as God shows them to me. Otherwise you'll find your reading has been wasted; three days later all that exciting stuff God showed you will have been forgotten! My marking system varies, but is basically very simple. I underline verses that leap out at me and squeeze comments in the margin. Sometimes I put in a short reference by the side of verses that I want to compare. For example, if I'm reading John's gospel and it keeps striking me that Jesus never did anything without his Father's permission, I'll put the letters SUBN, for submission, against verses such as John 5:19; John 5:30; John 8:28; etc. Or I'll ring each time Jesus calls God Father (that is more than 120!). That way you have a record of what God said to you for future use but without the need for masses of notes. I find that I tend to lose separate notes anyway!

From reading to studying

This is taking us more into the realm of Bible study, and for that it's necessary to equip yourself with a few more tools. Some people find a notebook helpful here. I suggest you buy exercise books and keep them all together, rather than using loose leaves and losing them all round your room! I suppose the minimum for Bible study is a pen, something to write notes in (either a Bible or a notebook), a concordance and a good commentary. And a Bible, of course! A concordance is basically a word list which will help you find where any verse is in the Bible. I would recommend the New International Version or the Good News Concordance.

A good commentary (and no more expensive than a pair of trousers or a visit to the hairdresser) is *The New Bible Commentary* (published by Inter-Varsity Press). As with Bible notes, remember it's Bible first, commentary second. A third useful aid is *The New Bible Dictionary*, also published by IVP which is exactly what it sounds like.

Bible study should go beyond your normal quiet time. It should go deeper, when you deliberately learn about biblical issues and characters, so that you get the feel of the word of God. After all the Bible is called the sword of God, and you need to practise wielding it! Bible study is supposedly easier for 'professionals' like me: we have to do it to prepare for preaching and so on. So could you. One way to discipline yourself to do Bible study is to make sure you have an outlet for your studies, so that you too have to prepare, perhaps for your church Bible study, or your school or work Christian Union. Otherwise, a book such as *Search the Scriptures* might help, or even a correspondence course. Some addresses are listed at the back of this book of places which do suitable courses. Or choose a subject yourself that interests you (God as Father, healing, the Peace Movement) and study it from the Bible.

Think on....

Lastly in this chapter, what about Bible meditation? It's a phrase that is currently being bandied about, and I know I've needed to unpack it and see what it means. You can immediately dismiss any ideas about Eastern meditation and mystic trances, because at best that's cranky, and at worst it's actually occultic and dangerous.

Christian meditation does *not* involve blanking your mind out, or turning inside and seeing what lies within you, or endlessly (and mindlessly) repeating a phrase or word—the Eastern mantra. Christian meditation is specifically meditation on the word of God, the Bible (or on Jesus himself, or on God as revealed in creation). So how is it different from Bible reading or Bible study?

I recently went out for a meal with the family I live with to celebrate someone's birthday. We went to a local 'carvery'. It's the kind of place where you pay a set amount (only £5!) and then help yourself, buffet-style, to the starter, main course, and sweet. I'll make a confession—at things like that I always go mad over the starter (it's called greed!) and then have little room left for the rest. On the way back from collecting my bread, salad, pâté, prawns, pickle, etc. I passed a man who had had the good sense to take a selective but not excessive portion of just prawns and salad. In retrospect I'm sure he had the right idea, probably suffered less from indigestion, and enjoyed what he did have more.

Bible meditation works on the same principle. It takes a small portion (one or two verses) of Scripture, and savours it slowly and lovingly. Meditation is the chewing over and slow appreciation of the word of God. It follows my mum's basic guide to good eating—eat slowly, and don't talk with your mouth full!

It's for you!

That takes us to the 'how?' of meditation. I normally choose just one or two verses of the Bible and memorize them by saying them four or five times. Memory is vital to meditation, because once it's committed to memory you can meditate at any odd time during the day, even if you've only got a spare five minutes between lessons or at a bus stop! So I might be looking at John 1:14 or Colossians 1:18 or Matthew 4:19–20. Then, when there's no distraction around, or when I'm doing something that doesn't demand my full concentration (no, not homework!) I begin quietly and slowly to meditate on the verses. Now what that means for me is that I think over *each* word of the verse. Why is that particular word used and not another? Is there an emphasis that I've missed before? Once I've gone over every word and its shades of meaning, I ask the Holy Spirit to help my mind to wander! Normally I don't have any problems in this area—my mind wanders quite freely and easily, and usually when I'm meant to be praying! But, in meditation, I ask God the Holy Spirit to *lead* my mind in 'spiritual imagination' and I follow it.

Take, for example, Matthew 4:19–20. First, I'd examine the phrase 'He said'—the spoken word of command from Jesus. 'He....' Jesus the supreme example of a man. 'He said'—actually in the Greek that's present tense 'He *says*', so it's more immediate, or first hand, as told by eye witness. And it's what he still says. And so on. Then I'd start to wander spiritually around the verse. 'Follow me.' Where to? That must have taken faith. Why didn't Jesus reveal where to? 'Fishers of men.' That means people who catch fish (or men) and not just interest or influence them. People who know when, where and how to catch, people who use the right bait. And so on.

Getting straight to the point

And lastly, why meditate? Because it's the smallest, best digested and easiest handled slice of the bread of life, and it's basic to your spiritual diet. It takes time and practice to acquire the art, but you can't afford not to. It's the spiritual equivalent of an intravenous drip! It gets the food to where it's needed (your spirit) in the quickest way. It helps you handle, understand, love and memorize the word of God. Above all else, it's a quick means to an end—it shows you much of Jesus. The results of meditation are eternal and can never be taken from you (Proverbs 4:4–5).

So there it is, the mystery debunked. One more thing—as you read, study and meditate on the Bible, remember it's God's word to you. So he'll help you read it. Set your face towards God, and encourage your heart in prayer to pant after God so that you feel thirsty for more of him, and then reading the Bible, studying and meditating will come all the more easily. You might take it a book at a time. You might use Bible reading notes. You might try reading through the whole Bible. (After all, who wants to meet with Nehemiah and confess they never read his book?!) But whatever you do, do it now, keep at it, and enjoy it!

3
Turning on the Power Supply

Practical Prayer and Praise

I'm told that one of my (many) infuriating habits is that in times of physical stress or awkwardness, I have the irritating quirk of suddenly seeing the absurdity of the situation, and bursting out laughing. You may think it's a good thing to be able to laugh at moments of crisis or danger, but some of my friends and colleagues will tell you that there's a time and a place. And halfway up a steep staircase with a very heavy filing cabinet caught on the banister is neither the time nor the place for fits of semi-hysterical laughter! Neither is the bottom of a dinghy on the Norfolk Broads, with the sail and rudder wrapped round your legs and a motor launch heading straight for you!

A sense of the absurd

I can't help it. You could say it's hysteria or fear transference, but I prefer to think it's an optimistic sense of the absurd. Sometimes I'm struck with the same sort of sense when, at the end of an evangelistic meeting, be it a cabaret, a coke bar, concert or whatever, I close with a prayer of challenge to commitment. I know it's a serious and important moment, but occasionally the viewpoint of your average non-Christian comes across, and there's just a touch of the absurd.

There you are, everyone else in this room is listening, but you are standing out at the front. So far you've been talking with and to them, and hopefully most of them have been listening. But now, suddenly, you close your eyes, and start talking out loud to this person whom you can neither see, hear, touch or smell! Peculiar, isn't it?

And prayer *can* seem that strange to someone unused to it. Nearly everyone prays at some time or other. Even hard-headed, super cool fifth formers in East London will admit that when asked in class. Usually it's in the form of one of three basic prayers. Either emergency prayers, 'Oh God, help, I've got an exam tomorrow'; bargain prayers, 'If you get me past this bunch of skinheads I promise to quit bunking R.E.'; or occasionally relief prayers, 'Thank God that copper didn't stop me.' Unfortunately these types of prayers are usually as well aimed as a space-shuttle launched satellite! You don't really know where they're going—as Paul explained in Acts 17:22–34.

The language of love

When a person becomes a Christian, he has to learn that prayer is a vital part of a relationship between him and God, and that doesn't necessarily come naturally. Some people suffer for *years* because of this common assumption that prayer is automatic for the Christian. So in this chapter I'd like to look at the subject of prayer, and because the two are so closely bound together we shall also look a little at praise and worship. That's another source of sometimes acute embarrassment for the younger growing Christian. And sometimes for us older ones too!

The Bible, realistic as ever, holds no illusions about the difficulties of prayer and praise. Paul is constantly encouraging Christians to pray at all times for all things and for all people, and to praise God in all circumstances (sometimes despite circumstances as in Philippians 4:4–7). Paul was great at encouraging people, but he could also state the case pretty plainly too. And on prayer he does just that. Romans

8:26–27 is clear; we *don't* know how to pray. The early disciples at least had the guts to ask Jesus how to pray, and so he takes the trouble in Matthew 6 and 7 to tell them, and not to presume that they knew.

What is prayer? It's the direct communication between you and your God, *and vice versa*. If you've ever played a variation on Chinese whispers, you'll know how very important direct communication is. You know the kind of thing I mean. One person sends out the message, 'Send reinforcements, we're going to advance.' And it gets passed down the line, person to person, whispered into listening ears, and then finally received and reported as, 'Send three and fourpence, we're going to a dance'. That's supposed to have actually happened in World War 2. I don't know about that but the principle holds good. Unless you have *direct* access to God for yourself, his message to you will be garbled, and you'll no longer have a relationship, only a long distance passing acquaintance.

The vital link

That works both ways equally, of course. The Bible makes it clear (1 Timothy 2:5) that there is only one mediator between you and God, and that's Jesus who prays for us at the right hand of God the Father. God wants to hear from you, and he does it through Jesus alone. Others can pray for you and with you, but that's a bonus. You have to have that link yourself to develop the love relationship.

When I was at school I fell out with one of my mates, and for a while did the usual stupid 'Coventry act'. Using a middle-man as go-between, we passed messages backwards and forwards, 'Tell Eddie that if he wants his pen back he'll have to ask for it.' 'Tell Pete that it's my pen and if he doesn't give it to me right now I'll punch him in the throat!' That's pathetic if it's between friends; it's tragic if it's between you and God. Prayer is talking and listening to God for *yourself*. Even if at first it seems a little absurd.

Starting off

Most conversations struck up between potential friends start
with the general: the weather, football, fashion, music. Then
it soon moves to the specific, and you talk about what you
think or like about that team, or this record. From there, if
you like the person, you usually begin to listen to what they
like and think. The pattern is the same with talking to God.
We usually start the relationship with the general: how good
he is, how pleased we are Jesus died for us. Then we get on to
what we are really interested in: our dreams, needs, fears.
And usually last, we begin to learn to listen to what God
thinks is important about us, our lives, what pleases him,
what hurts him, what *his* plans are for us. I suppose that's
really the stage when we stop having good ideas and just ask
God to 'bless' them (whatever that means!) and instead ask
God for his plans, knowing that they'll be the best.

What to say

But what should you say when you pray? Answer—anything.
Only be real and honest. Use plain language that you feel at
home with (bearing in mind that if you start swearing at God
you'll soon start to feel pretty rotten, because that's a sign of
anger and lack of respect in your heart). Thees and thous will
probably not come naturally (although remember for some
people, particularly older people, that *is* the kind of language
they feel at home with). Tell God how you feel. Tell him how
you want to feel. Tell him why. Tell him what he's like. Not
because he doesn't know already; but in any love relationship
it's right and natural to want to show love and affection, to
express love. I like to tell my earthly dad that I love him and
appreciate him and enjoy his love for me. It should be the
same only more so with my heavenly Dad. This is certainly
part of praising God in prayer, but there is more.

In spirit and in truth

Everyone has their own style of praise and worship. Sometimes those styles are reflected denominationally, so a Pentecostal church will often include more choruses, hand clapping, dancing and arm raising than a Brethren church. It's not that one style is necessarily better than another. What is vital is that praise and worship is from your spirit and is real. Jesus said that God is worshipped in spirit and in truth (John 4:23). Romans 12:1–2 makes it clear that we worship God with our whole lives, not just by singing hymns on a Sunday morning. So what's real for you is what's right for you, provided you're always looking to go deeper in praise and worship, and to learn new things, because God is always doing new things.

Some years ago when visiting the late David Watson's church in York, I first experienced people raising their hands to God in worship. It was a natural and real response, saying to God, 'Here I am, take me, I'm yours.' It was a scriptural response, lifting holy hands to God (as is dancing), but I'm afraid at the time it wasn't for me. I remember remarking to a friend next to me, 'If ever you see me doing that, I'm faking it!' To say 'if ever' was a bit rash, but at the time it was true enough. Now that was O.K. but I'm afraid the problem was that I also judged those who were dancing and raising their arms in praise. I judged them to be show-offs, attention seekers or weird fanatics. Perhaps some were. But most weren't. I've had to ask God to forgive me that judgement. And eventually God led me to a place and a time when it was real and right for me to praise him in similar ways.

So find in praise and worship what's real and right for you. Don't worship in public in a way you wouldn't worship at home. Don't be intimidated by anyone around you, and don't intimidate anyone around you. Then learn to appreciate the different expressions of worship and praise. And, of course, in one sense, the more you can join in for real, the greater the bonus to you, and to God.

Godward not manward

It took me ages before I'd dance to the Lord in praise. I'm not a natural dancer, and when I do dance all the excess fat that I like to think is muscle tends to be shown up for what it really is! But then, I'm not dancing for other people, I'm dancing for God's pleasure. And dancing has a way of involving your whole body in praise to him. I can't play an instrument, and my voice isn't too great either, but like praying, worship is not manward, it's Godward, and he made me without mistakes. Whatever I'm like, he loves me, even enough to change me, so I get on with it! I use praise tapes, or records to sing to or dance to in my own quiet times. They help me to worship quietly or praise loudly. I'll sing and speak in tongues; I'll even dance in my room on my own in my quiet time! Praising Almighty God is exciting, and most descriptions in the Bible are pretty noisy ones! Perhaps we should be having 'noisy times' as well as 'quiet times'!

You might try the same sort of thing for yourself, and when it's real and important enough in your own quiet time, you'll soon find it's spilling over into your church, or your Christian Union, or your church youth group. Praise and worship is a helpful springboard into the main subject of this chapter—prayer, which I intend to get back to right away!

Owning up

God also wants us to own up to things in prayer. In the chapter on commitment I talked about the need for daily, ongoing repentance, and this is part of the Christian's prayer life. Again it's not that God doesn't know about what we thought/said/did/didn't do that was wrong. But he likes us to tell him. That way we learn honesty and humility, and God gets the opportunity directly to forgive us and cleanse us (1 John 1:9) so we don't keep doing the same things wrong again and again.

Letting God in

I'm fortunate. My parents expect me to tell them if I'm in difficulty or under particular pressure, say at work. If I needed help and didn't ask, they'd be hurt and upset, and I'd lose out too. Again, that natural relationship between parent and child mirrors the supernatural. God wants us to ask him for help whenever we need it. I used to think (and I can remember arguing about this one over cooked Sunday breakfast with Mum) that God didn't want to be bothered with the little hassles of life, so he left us to get on with them. Well, sometimes he does, but never without wanting and waiting to help and be involved. Matthew 6:25–34 is the true perspective on this.

Just across the road from where I live in East London is a sorting office. If ever the postman calls to deliver a parcel to me and I'm not in, he leaves a card so that I can collect the package at the sorting office. Sometimes I think God is forced to act like that. Somewhere in a big sorting office in heaven is a room full of parcels marked 'for Pete Gilbert', and I never collected them because I didn't think God would be bothered to give me the answer to that particular problem. I was out too often when he called. Prayer makes sure you ask for help, and listening makes sure you receive it.

Not that God is like some big fruit machine in the sky, just there to dole out easy answers and glittery prizes, if I put in the right prayer and pull the handle! That's what a lot of young non-Christian people at school think prayer is, and why they're disappointed when it doesn't work. The prayers that get answered are the real prayers, the ones that look for relationship and not just jackpots. The prayers that *always* get answered are those prayed in line with God's will for your life, those which will be best for you and those around you. Yes, it's true to say that every prayer gets an answer: 'yes', 'no' or 'wait'. But that *can* be a cop-out. God would rather teach me how to pray so that he can say 'yes', because that's his desire.

So when you've praised in prayer, and repented in prayer,

here are a few things I've found useful in asking for things in prayer.

Prayer and your perspective

First, take a step back from the need. If you pray when feeling heavily burdened yourself (as opposed to feeling God's heart on the matter), then you'll probably end the prayer time feeling depressed and faithless. You prayed before and nothing's changed. You're even developing an expectation of failure, a kind of negative faith that nothing will happen! Prayer that leads to depression or frustration is going wrong somewhere. So step back from the problem, and begin to praise God for who he is and not what he can do. If necessary, praise as *an act of will* as David instructs his soul to do in Psalm 103. As you praise God in this way it will become real in your feelings too. This is vital, because what you see (and believe for) in prayer depends on the position you pray from. If you pray from problem and defeat, that's all you see. If you pray from a vision of Jesus and victory, that's what you get. It's like the difference between crossing noisy, smelly, congested London by car, or flying high above it by aeroplane. Always ask for things from above looking down on the problem (God's perspective) and not from under the problem looking up (our natural perspective, to Satan's delight). Pray from faith, and not unbelief.

Ask before you ask

Next, pray about what to pray about! You may think you know what the issues are to pray over, but they may not be the root, and you'll end up wasting your time and God's. This often happens in counselling situations, when the 'presenting problem' that the person comes with isn't the real issue. I remember a lad of seventeen talking to me after a concert when God had spoken to him, telling me he had a real problem with swearing. I could have prayed for self-control for him but God managed to get through to me that

that wasn't the issue. Listening to God with one ear and the lad with the other, it became clear that the swearing was only a symptom of a deeper anger and resentment, mainly because the lad's father had left home, and therefore the lad had a lousy picture of what God is like as a father. I had to pray about what to pray about, then listen for the answer.

Learning to listen

Listening isn't always easy. It's not as super-spiritual as it sounds, however. What I do is get alone in my room as quiet as possible. Then I ask God a direct question. People questioned God all the time in the Bible (see Isaiah 6:11 or Habakkuk 1:2). Having asked the question, I wait. I think about the question with my eyes closed to avoid distractions, and I think about Jesus and his ability to get through to me even at my thickest. As with Bible meditation, my mind will wander, but I deliberately keep it spiritual! God may bring to mind a past experience where he taught me a lesson. Or a Bible verse. Or a personal situation to pray for. I may see a picture in my mind and begin to pray around that. Or I may 'feel' rather than 'hear' what God is saying. Whatever I get, I trust that if I ask to hear, God will do his bit and speak. It's not difficult, but like everything else, it takes a bit of practice.

In Jesus' name

The lovely thing about praying about what to pray about is that when you have heard from God, you can then pray in absolute faith and confidence, knowing that it's in God's will. And *whatever* you ask in God's will, the Father will give you, because you can ask it in the name of Jesus. There's nothing magical about tagging 'in Jesus' name' on the end of a prayer, but it'll work one hundred per cent if it really is asking 'into (the exact Greek) the name of Jesus' (John 16:23). The reason is that you can't ask anything in Jesus' name *really* unless it is God's will, because Jesus never did anything that's not his Father's will. (See John 5:19; John

5:30: John 7:16; John 8:28.) So once God has told you what to pray, pray with boldness in the name of his Son and the answer will be 'Yes!' Prayer draws on a blank cheque, which is drawn on heaven's reserves, cashed on earth and signed by Jesus Christ.

To be precise

When repenting or asking in prayer, practise being specific. I'd prayed for years that God would bless Auntie so and so, and to be honest, I never really knew if he answered, because I never really knew what I was asking for. God must get so frustrated with some of my woollier prayers. I can picture him saying, 'I'll do it, but what is it that you want?' I'm learning to be specific in my prayers, so I get specific answers. That way God also builds my faith. If I need £50 (notice I said *need*) and ask him for £50, when he gives it to me I can recognize his provision, and next time when I need £75, I'll have more faith to believe him for it. Keep a record of your prayer requests. I guarantee it will amaze you from month to month as you see what God has done through and for you. It will also help you to keep praying when the answer is slow in coming, although beware praying for years on end without seeing some fruit or results. That may mean you need to adjust your methods of praying. It's right to be persistent (Luke 11:8; Luke 18:1–8), but it's also right to expect to see results (John 15:8). God wants fruitfulness as well as faithfulness.

Prayer in action

That brings me to another interesting point. Your prayer life will often cause you to be more involved in the answer, not less. I sometimes promise to prayed for someone when I don't really want to do anything else. Forget it! Prayer is dangerous, because often God will say, 'You prayed, now you are part of the answer!' In Matthew 9:36—10:1 you see a perfect example. Jesus commands his disciples to pray to

God for workers for the human harvest. Presumably they do so. Then immediately in Matthew 10:1 Jesus sends for them to answer their own prayer! I'll bet that was a bit of a shock! Faith without action is dead (James 2:17) and so is prayer without action.

Change the fuse

The point is this: real prayer will require you to change. God never removes problems, he deals with people. With you and me. 1 Peter 4:17 says that judgement starts with the family of God. At college I used to pray, 'Lord, make my fellow Christians in this hall of residence really love each other because they don't.' Eventually I stopped long enough to hear God get a word in! 'I will, and I'll start with you. You don't love enough, so how about it?' was the drift of what he said.

Sometimes we pray for something and God can't answer because to do so he'd need to channel too much spiritual power through us in order to shift the problem. We've turned on the power supply, but it's as though we're trying to run an electric fire on a three-amp fuse. Something's going to blow! So sometimes God's first job after you've prayed is to enlarge the 'fuse' capacity of your spiritual life, so that you can take more of a Holy Spirit charge to do the job and get the prayer answered. That means readjustment in your own life. It means dross coming to the surface. It can mean pain and battle. It will also mean ultimate victory.

Pray in the Spirit

If you've ever wondered, like I have, why such a fuss is sometimes made about speaking in tongues, there are a couple of points I'd like to mention here. The first is that during praise, when you're praying to God and telling him how good he is, you can use the gift of tongues to increase your vocabulary! That will increase the sense of joy and excitement in you, as well as please God, and it's a vital part of praise praying. The other reason tongues are important is that sometimes, when you're praying for someone or against a particular strategy of the enemy (Ephesians 6:12), you don't know exactly what or how to pray. At those times the Holy Spirit can communicate direct with your spirit as you pray in tongues, and that's a very powerful prayer weapon.

Pulling a 'fast one'

While we're looking at how to ask for things in prayer, let me throw in the idea of fasting. It's not an idea that comes naturally to me; I enjoy food, and there has to be a good reason for me to miss a meal! Fasting *is* a good reason. Although there are no short cuts to becoming spiritually mature, fasting is the nearest thing I've come to one. It's an idea from the Old Testament, which Jesus obviously expected his disciples to carry over into the New Testament, since he refers to '*whenever* you fast' in Matthew 6:16, not '*if* you fast'. (Interestingly enough he does the same thing with tithing. More about that later!) The biblical fast was in periods of twenty-four hours and usually meant an abstinence from food, not necessarily from drink. The benefits of fasting are that it's good (not bad) for your system medically. It has the effect of what my mother used to call 'a good dose of salts'—it clears out the system! That means fewer spots, whiter eyes, healthier hair, and it might also mean weight loss. It's also good for you spiritually. Mealtimes can become prayer times, and since your body clock will tell you when it is mealtime, you have a built-in reminder to pray! Also it's wonderful how not eating sharpens your senses! You become more alert, less sleepy. You have more time to pray. And, of course, fasting tells God that you mean business over the issue that you're fasting about. You're not twisting his arm to make him answer. It's more like a present, a sacrifice you willingly make in obedience and an indication that you are serious about God's will on earth. It's nice that we have a God who is close enough to receive the presents we offer him.

Hard and 'fast' rules

Of course, there are some simple rules to follow. Don't try a forty-day fast straight off! Start by missing just one meal. Next week try missing two. Aim in the third week for a full twenty-four hours, perhaps from tea-time one day to tea-time the next. And do take plenty of liquid, though not tea or coffee. You might be surprised how addicted you can get to tea and coffee, and may even experience initial withdrawal symptoms of headaches. I usually drink hot diluted orange squash when I'm fasting. Don't fast if you're ill or run down. When you do fast, fast over a specific issue, one at a time. And it's good to establish a regular pattern, fasting perhaps one day a week, decreasing time spent eating, increasing time spent praying. It's amazing how many young Christians leave this whole area to others. Don't. Fasting and praying is for *you*. If you don't believe me, ask God. And you might also want to look at an excellent book by Arthur Wallis called *God's Chosen Fast*.

Praying aloud

Whenever I think of this next area of prayer, I usually squirm a bit. Have you ever been in public prayer meetings with long, embarrassing silences? Or perhaps you have been at the school C.U. meeting where a professional pray-er has gone on and on for ages. Have you ever been in the situation of people waiting for you to pray and you haven't been able to? It can be really awful. On the other hand, I've been to prayer meetings that have been exciting, and taught me a lot about God and prayer. I've listened in awe as the Holy Spirit has led the prayers, so that there's a real flow, a real sense of purpose and direction. If you're going to take advantage of this kind of unique privilege and even be involved, there are 'ways in'.

When I go swimming in the local outdoor pool, I always dive straight in. I can't bear the idea of slowly lowering myself down the steps. But some people find jumping in too great a shock to the system. It's the same with public praying. Either launch straight in and get on with it, if you're an extrovert, or lower yourself into it gradually, if you're scared, shy, or embarrassed. But one thing you shouldn't do, and that's just stand around watching.

Every Christian has at least one thing to thank God for. So why not start the prayer off, 'Thank you God for....' and then say the one thing and finish. Or, 'I want to ask you God for...' and mention one request and then stop. Some Christian Unions I've visited sit in a circle, and each person prays for the one on their left. Or if they don't want to pray, they just say 'Amen'. Of course, that gets silly if you get a circle of people all saying 'Amen' one after the other!

By the way, this word 'Amen' is a Hebrew word, and all it means is, 'yes, God, that's right,' or 'Let it happen like that God.' It's not magical, but it's useful to show you agree. (If you don't agree with a prayer, then don't say Amen.) Jesus made it clear that if two or more met together to pray that he'd be there, and if they agreed together in him it would be done. So praying together and agreeing, or 'amening', together is important. And it lets you know when the other guy's finished!

Willing and able

I'm presuming two things in all of this. One...that you do know God yourself. But if you don't that doesn't stop you praying. To the non-Christian, God will prove that Jesus is Lord, and your prayer can be asking for just that. To the Christian God says, 'Prove to me that my Jesus is your Lord.' The Christian's prayer life then will reflect that, and build a relationship upon it. Two...I'm presuming that you do want to pray on your own and out loud. If you don't want to pray, and you are a Christian, then there's a serious block somewhere, and it'll come down to sin. If that's the case, go back to the chapter on commitment and the Holy Spirit. That's really the chapter for you, and not this one just yet!

4

'Yet Without Sin'

Escape Routes from Temptation

There was a time on his radio and TV shows when comedian Les Dawson would play a selection of well-known tunes on the piano. The trouble was he played them slightly off key. Not enough to make the tune unrecognizable, but just enough to make it sound terrible! I'm told by piano players that it's actually quite difficult to play that badly out of tune.

When you come to look at this whole area of temptation, Les Dawson and his off-key piano becomes a useful picture. He knew exactly which notes to hit to produce that off-key cacophony. And that's what your enemy and mine, the devil, does with us when it comes to temptation. He knows that if he 'plays' certain notes in our life, then the 'chords' of our desires, lusts and selfish ambitions will respond in a jarring discord. If ever Satan calls the tune in your life, you can be sure it will sound horrible. And unfortunately, he's very good at knowing just where we're weakest. So he plays on our weaknesses, our own inside wrong desires, and they eventually surface in an ugly din. It's just like it says in James 1:14–15, 'each one is tempted when, by his own evil desire, he is dragged away and enticed. Then, after desire has conceived, it gives birth to sin; and sin, when it is full-grown, gives birth to death.' If God wants us to be well-tuned instruments for his praise, blending with the orchestra of his

57

family, Satan wants us to be an out-of-tune, toneless one-man band.

Be prepared. I know when it comes to temptation, I need to be very clear in my heart as to what's going on, because once the pressure is on and I'm being tempted, there's no time or breathing space to suss out what or why. It's often all I can do just not to sin, so before you get bogged down by temptation and it spills over into sin, let's look at some basics on this whole subject.

What is temptation?

Straight off, what is temptation? I've hinted already that it's those inside tugs that pull us away from what we know is right to do that which we know is wrong but which we still like to do. On my car radio there's a button marked AFC that's supposed to keep the radio homed in on the station I'm tuned to. The closer you get to God, the finer tuned you are to receive what he says, thinks and feels. Temptation strikes a nasty chord inside us and tries to pull us 'off station' away from God.

O.K. So obviously it's not a particularly nice thing. But we're surrounded by temptation in one form or another all day—circumstances, advertising posters, TV, newspapers and so on. And what's worse, we find something inside us wanting to respond to these external stimuli. No wonder Paul wrote in Romans 7:15, 'What I want to do I do not do, but what I hate I do.' But the good news is he didn't stop there; there's a way out of the problem so that temptation does not have to lead to sin. That's why he wrote Romans 7:24–25 and chapter 8.

We also need to be clear about the origin of temptation. It's based on the gift of free will, which God gave to his created beings, men and angels alike. Satan and his lot chose to rebel against God and later tempted Adam and Eve to do the same. Without freedom of choice there could be no temptation. Temptation prompts us to choose against God, and temptation is never from God. The occasional use of the word in the Bible (for example, Matthew 6, 'lead us not into temptation') in relation to God are examples of bad translation. Matthew 6 is more accurately translated 'lead us not to the time of testing or trial'. Temptation is from Satan, not from God. James is clear about this in James 1:12–13. God is our heavenly Father who only gives good gifts (James 1:17).

Why is it allowed?

But if God is so good, why doesn't he get rid of all temptation and evil right now? It's allowed because God won't contradict his own character. Because God is love (1 John 4:16), he'll never force his will on you. As long as there is choice, there will be temptation. God can't do better than send his Son Jesus to beat the hold of sin on you and me, so that temptation need not lead to sin and death. And let's face it, if God destroyed all temptation and evil at noon today, who'd be left at 12.01? Not me. Not you. Out of love our holy God delays the ending of all evil, sin and suffering on earth even though it wracks him with anguish and crucified his Son, because 'he is unwilling that any should perish' (2 Peter 3:9). This is why temptation is allowed.

In fact, God will even use it for good. He can use temptation to refine you and tune you in to himself better. He'll use all things for good if you trust him (Romans 8:28) and temptation resisted builds the character of Jesus in you (1 Peter 1:6–7).

So who gets tempted?

I don't really need to detail what temptation is and what it feels like since we all know what it's like, because we all get tempted. Whoever your spiritual 'hero' is (and I do hope you have someone you admire in Jesus) from Martin Luther through Calvin to the latest Spring Harvest speaker, they've all been tempted. And will be again! I've been tempted. And so have you. There are no exceptions. And that includes the ultimate, perfect example, the spiritual hero beyond all other comparisons: Jesus Christ himself (Hebrews 4:15). That's why he's the perfect example. What would be the point of loving Jesus, the God Man, and letting his Spirit change us to be like him, if he'd never experienced all the hassles, trials and temptations that are part and parcel of our everyday lives, and if he hadn't beaten them all? Jesus lived the kind of life that we were meant for. Abundant life here on earth. That's the only way he could show us exactly what we were meant to be like.

Temptation and sin: the difference

Now if everyone, including Jesus, has been tempted, then we get neatly to the next important point. The Bible is equally clear that not only was Jesus tempted in every respect like we are, but he was also *without sin*. It, therefore, becomes clear that temptation and sin are two completely different things. To be tempted (as Jesus was) is not automatically to sin (as Jesus didn't). That may seem a very simple thing to say, but loads of Christians carry terrible burdens of guilt because they fail to make this distinction between temptation and sin. Young Christians in particular are afflicted by temptations in their thought-life, and although many may never stray from thoughts to action, they end up feeling condemned, constantly reminded about Jesus' words about the danger of sinning in thought as well as deed (Matthew 5:27–28). But the key words here are those that indicate motive. If you look at a girl deliberately in order to lust after her, then that's sin, not temptation. Jesus equates that with the actual deed of adultery, because the deed is only the end result of motive and desire from the heart. So just what is the difference between temptation and sin?

Let's look at one example. If you're a bloke, and walking down the street you're suddenly confronted by a sexually explicit advertising poster designed to arouse you, your immediate reaction will be temptation and not sin. But if you then *deliberately* look at it again, your motives are wrong and you've moved from temptation to sin. It's like crossing a fine line, best distinguished between a first look and a second look! And it's no good just saying, 'Oh well then, I'll make the first look last longer!' The first tug which pulls your thoughts/eyes/feet in the direction of sin is the common experience of humanity. It was common to Jesus. It is temptation. And it carries no condemnation from God (Romans 8:1) so it shouldn't from you either. In God's sight you're not guilty because you're tempted. You need to learn where the difference between temptation and sin lies. The crossover line becomes more clearly marked the 'finer tuned' you are to God. Hence our need to keep a good relationship through prayer, Bible reading, worship and fellowship. And remember *playing* with temptation isn't temptation at all, it's sin.

Escape routes

I'd like to offer you a very simple biblical model for dealing with temptation that works in my own experience. You may need to make adjustments to make it work for you. First, you'll never be a helpless victim of temptation if you're a Christian. Temptation no longer has to lead to bondage where sin is its inevitable result. God has promised that there will always be an escape route. Apparently one of the hardest parts about trying to escape from the old penal colony on Devil's Island was overcoming the daunting effects of its reputation of being escapeproof! Let the word be spread that a successful escape had taken place, and half the difficulty is over, because people begin to realize that escape is on the cards after all! Temptation works the same way. Once you realize that there is always a way out that avoids sin, you're on the road to dealing with the rest of the problem. I have memorized the promise and use it as ammunition against the enemy when I am tempted. I suggest that you do the same. 1 Corinthians 10:13 says it all!

Reckon yourself

Next, how do you find the escape route already promised? There's a word used in Romans 6:11 that I caught on to some time ago—'*Reckon* yourself dead to sin.' While at college some eight years ago, when God was dealing radically with my life I read Watchman Nee's book *The Normal Christian Life*. I found this really mind-blowing. Romans 6 is so rich and deep you could read it time and again and still discover new truths to live by. You and I *died* with Jesus on the cross. In some incredible way the pattern of our old life of 'temptation that leads to sin' was killed. This isn't wishful thinking, it's spiritual fact. The whipping post saw potential for healing bought; the cross saw potential for death to your old self; the blood of Jesus saw potential for spiritual cleansing; and the resurrection saw potential for new life. So when you're next tempted, think of the cross of Jesus Christ and remember that you hung there too because of Jesus. Reckon yourself dead to sin. You are to consider yourself beyond its influence, in Jesus. If you have any doubt that you are dead to sin, then you accept the lies of the enemy ('the father of lies' John 8:44) and start to live them out through sin in the face of God's Son, who died on the cross to nail down your 'old self'. I'm not saying pretend you don't feel tempted. I am saying *reckon* yourself dead to sin—sin will not automatically follow the temptation that you feel. You won't stop the devil shouting (though eventually he'll tire and grow hoarse), but you needn't reply. Temptation no longer leads to sin.

Resisting

Recap—there's always an escape route. Its entrance is found by reckoning yourself dead to sin. Next, you progress down the escape route by resisting. James 4:7 has a double command, 'Submit yourselves, then, to God. Resist the devil, and he will flee from you.' Resist the devil when you're tempted, but do it in the right way, or he'll wipe the floor with you.

In Greek legend there was a monster called the Medusa, the Gorgon. She looked human enough, except for her incredibly ugly face and snakish hair! If you faced her, you turned to stone, so understandably it was a bit difficult to defeat her! Eventually some bloke had the nouse to fight her without looking directly at her—he only watched her reflection through his polished shield. Now you and I could learn a thing or two here. Our shield is a shield of faith in our God (Ephesians 6:16) and is able to quench every fiery dart (temptation) of the enemy. You don't resist the devil by fighting him face to face...he'll win hands down every time. You resist the devil by submitting to God first. Let God do the fighting on your behalf.

How does this work? You know for yourself that if you're tempted to eat more than you should, or go too far sexually with your boy/girl friend, or spend more money than you should that the more you concentrate on the temptation, the more it looms in your mind and the harder it is to ignore. It's no good turning to the enemy and grappling with him and saying through clenched teeth, 'I will *not* do that, it's wrong. I won't, I won't, I...whoops!!' Before you know where you are, concentrating on the problem and fighting the enemy direct has lost you the battle. So what to do? 'Submit yourselves then, to God.' Don't struggle with the enemy. Just walk straight into the presence of God (Hebrews 10:19) and tell him with honesty you're being tempted. If the old landlord of your life (the devil) tries to regain his old property (you!), don't fight him; take him to court to see the new Landlord (Jesus) who also happens to be Judge and King. You'll be dragging Satan kicking and screaming into the presence of Almighty God and his Son. And because good and evil, love and hate, light and dark don't mix, before you know it, by first submitting yourself to God, you'll have *resisted* the devil, and he'll have run off! So next time that Satan whispers, 'Wouldn't you like to have sex right now with that person?' don't turn to him and say, 'I'm not going to listen to you Satan. I'm not even going to think about sex.' Instead turn your back on Satan and turn towards God and say, 'Father, right now I'm being tempted sexually and there's a pull in me to respond, but I'm looking at you, and I'm bringing Satan into your presence. I'm dead to sin through your Son Jesus, so will you please deal with our enemy?' Before you've finished the prayer, Satan will most likely have fled, and the temptation with it. Here's a diagram that might help explain what I've said.

What do you really want?

Of course, like all aspects of the Christian walk, God will operate from the desires of your heart. That means this will only work if you want to beat temptation and sin. If you don't want to be holy, you won't be, and then you need to ask God to make your heart pant after him more, to increase your desire to be holy because he is holy (1 Peter 1:15–16). Perhaps the chapter on commitment and the Holy Spirit will be helpful here?

Replacing

After reckoning and resisting, there comes replacing. You find Jesus uses this principle when tempted by Satan in the desert in Luke 4:1–13. Jesus resists by submitting himself to the word of God, and in addition, he deliberately replaces each of Satan's temptations with a greater and opposite truth. So when the temptation is 'turn stones to bread', Jesus replaces the temptation with 'man shall not live by bread alone'. When the temptation appeals to a desire for power and influence, Jesus counters it with an assertion that worship and service is due *only* to God. When the devil tries to tempt Jesus through pride or reputation, he warns Satan by reminding him of the command not to test God. The specific temptations of the enemy recorded here in Luke 4 mirror the types of temptation that befall us all (1 John 2:16). Each time Jesus' attitude *reckons* himself dead to sin, he *resists* Satan and *replaces* the temptation with a positive assertion.

It's easy to show how this works. Picture in your mind a tube of blue minty gel toothpaste. Think about the box it comes in; red with white writing. Think of the metal tube with its white plastic nozzle. Think of the clear, blue, minty gel itself. Think hard. Got it? Now stop thinking of it instantly! You must not think of blue minty gel toothpaste and tube! No, you mustn't even consider that fresh smell, that clear gel, that soft metal tube and cardboard box! Stop it!!

You see what I mean? It's hard to stop thinking about something on command. In fact, the more you're not supposed to think about it, the more you find you do. It's the same with that tempting thought. But supposing I said, 'Instead of thinking about blue minty gel toothpaste, think of a tall green tree, with wide branches and beautiful leaves rustling in the wind! A large brown trunk and swaying branches, shades of green, brown, gold and red, a magnificent oak or sycamore. Think hard! Picture it for yourself!'

You see? The toothpaste goes, the tree comes. Simple, but effective. You get rid of one thought not by fighting it to create a vacuum, but by ignoring it and replacing it with something else. You get rid of tempting thoughts by replacing them with good and pure thoughts. Whatever works best for you. I think about what heaven will be like. Or I picture Jesus as best I can. Or think about angels. And just to prove this principle not only works but is biblical, look at Philippians 4:8. Why not memorize a few verses to meditate on as part of your armoury of replacement?

I had a friend who carried a small notebook with suitable verses in it to replace his particular temptation. When tempted, he'd flick to the appropriate verse for a while, until he became so used to it he could remember it, by which time Satan had grown tired of trying that area of his life anyway. Constant readjustment in the battle against temptation and sin is necessary; Satan will keep trying and it stops you getting blasé or presumptive to have to keep resisting him in different areas.

Keep your distance!

And finally…I have left this point till last as it's so simple, but I guess it needs saying because I know how often I neglect it. Paul, writing to a young person concerning one particular temptation, gave sound working advice. 'Flee,' he said, 'the evil desires of youth' (2 Timothy 2:22). At the end of the day the easiest way to deal with temptation is not to put yourself in the way of it. In fact, do the opposite. Flee means run away from, not towards. There'll be some things that tempt you that you can, and therefore should, avoid altogether. So stay out of that newsagents! Don't go down that street with the provocative adverts! Avoid that particular group of people! And similarly, avoid tempting others! Otherwise *you* could be used as a tool in the hands of the enemy. Don't wear that particular blouse or pair of trousers! Don't tease that boy/girl friend physically in that way! Nobody gets away with breaking God's revealed ground rules. There are no 'special case mentalities'. Avoid temptation and sin that's already warned of in the Bible. Watch out for 'the evil desires of youth' or unequal yoking of Christian to non-Christian, or dishonest work practices, and so on. You know the areas in your life where you are prone to being tempted. Flee them!

Dealing with temptation with the right perspective can be fun. It's a challenge. It'll always be there, always changing. It's not sin. Beat it, and you'll grow more like Jesus. So use it as a doorway to maturity, and not a trapdoor to spiritual obscurity.

5

The Future Tense

God and Guidance

If you're honest, sometimes it's difficult to receive a gift. I know I like to get presents. But lots of people I know (me included) feel a bit embarrassed at receiving them. Fleeting thoughts go through your mind. 'I don't deserve this.' 'Do they really want to give me this?' 'Do I owe them something in return?' 'How do I say "thanks"?' The Bible says that it's more blessed to give than to receive, and sometimes it's easier as well!

It took me about seven years to discover that God's life in me is a gift. You've heard the clichés about Christianity being different from other religions because they search for God, while in Christianity God searches for man. Well, I never realized what massive implications that has if it's true. And here's some good news—it *is* true!

It's true that we can't please God because we're sinful—there's a disease inside that affects our thoughts, actions and motives. We know that when we choose God's cure—Jesus Christ—that that's a free gift of God's grace. The penalties of this disease are death—one hundred per cent fatality rate—and after that…judgement. Judgement would be getting what we deserve. Mercy would not be getting what we deserve. God's grace is getting what we don't deserve!

Now we know that in our heads, but often in our lives, we

try to be Christians in our own strength instead of carrying on receiving God's grace and forgiveness daily. It's a gift, but so often we try to deserve it—it's a basic fault of fallen people.

God's job to guide

So what's that got to do with guidance? Answer—everything. It's God's initiative to save us (Romans 5:8). It's God's initiative to keep us (Galatians 3:3) and it's God's initiative to guide us. I used to think guidance was something I had to chase after. As in a nightmare, I'd stumble after something I couldn't quite see, running in slow motion through porridge, and when I tried to grab this elusive thing called guidance, it would evaporate in my arms! A person could get very frustrated with God, chasing guidance like that! Lots of people do.

Let's get it really clear. God does the guiding. It's God's job to give and our job to receive. So the first thing to learn about guidance is that we can't earn God's acceptance, but we can receive it. We can't struggle for God's guidance, but we can receive it. God is the transmitter and man the receiver. A radio isn't complete in itself—it needs to be tuned in to the broadcast. It doesn't generate its own programmes, it receives them. You're not complete in yourself. You need to be tuned in to God.

If you've ever walked down the street with your ghetto-blaster, you'll know that radio reception is best with the aerial fine tuned. God's guidance is the same. Guidance is about relationship. It is not about a series of answers, or a set method to follow. It's about getting to know the guide. If you go orienteering, you trust the compass for direction. If you're after guidance, you need to trust God, so you've got to get to know him better (John 10:27). At least part of guidance is about growing in faith, taking risks. Even making mistakes. The finer tuned the relationship, the better the reception.

Our job to be guided

So though it's God's job, he's looking for our co-operation. More than we want to be guided, he wants to guide. And he knows how thick we can be. So he knows how best to get through to us. And that may be a different way for me than for you. But he wants your co-operation. God gave you a free will, because he wants a loving relationship with you, and he can't love a robot. In the same way, he'll guide you, when you put yourself in the way of guidance. That is why Romans 12:1–3 talks about a 'living sacrifice'. You have a daily, living choice. When your will crosses the revealed will of God, do you go God's way, or yours? That's relationship. It's also guidance.

But if guidance is about relationship, then shouldn't we be communicating more than we do? I don't just ask my dad's advice when I'm considering a job, or buying a car, when things get tough or confused. We talk about the everyday things too. Dad would guide me whether it was mending a bike or leaving home. 'If you then, though you are evil, know how to give good gifts to your children, how much more will your Father in heaven give good gifts to those who ask him! (Matthew 7:11). We need to get in the habit of asking God about everything, so that when the big questions come up, we've got the relationship and we know how it works. Practice may not make perfect, but it certainly helps!

Relationship, the key

This relationship thing is really the key in being guided. Realizing it's God's job to guide takes a whole load of strain off the subject. Building a relationship with God stops it being mechanical, makes it personal and fun. But there's another thing I've noticed in lots of younger Christians when I talk about guidance. They see guidance like a tightrope. You're at point A, heading for point B along a narrow, bouncy tightrope. One false step, one wrong decision, and you've fallen. That idea of guidance makes for very tense, insecure Christians. And it's not biblical. You're not on a tightrope of God's guidance that spans Satan's kingdom, as though God was playing games with you to see how far you'll get. The Bible says when you're a Christian you're smack in the middle of God's kingdom, taken out of the kingdom of darkness into the kingdom of light. The fact is, if you are being real and honest with God about wanting to be guided, then it's actually difficult for you to fall out of God's will. Don't let Satan tie you up with the old tightrope lie!

God copes with our mistakes

There's one more general point I want to make about guidance before we look at the practical 'hows'. I think it takes a lot of hassle away if we realize that God is big enough to cope with our mistakes, although that doesn't mean we don't need to bother getting it right in the first place (Romans 6:1). After all, if it's a love relationship we'll do all we can to please God. But it does mean that when we make mistakes (as opposed to deliberate rebellion) God can get us back on route without having to abandon us in a cul-de-sac, or give us second best. It's obvious in this world, as well as in your life, that God doesn't always have his way. He hates sin and pain and suffering, but they still happen because we're not robots. However, he will eventually get his way. Creation will be freed from the effects of our sin. So when I louse up guidance and get it wrong, God can cope. That's part of being one of his kids in his kingdom.

Mapping your route with God

You can check this for yourself from the Bible, but I don't believe God has a totally detailed blueprint for the whole of your life. I think he lays out the days and plans and knows what we'll choose to do and be (Psalm 139:13–16; Jeremiah 29:11–13). The details I think he expects us to work out with him willingly day by day, according to his principles of life. It's not that he isn't interested or involved, it's that he wants us to be interested and involved with him. Your heavenly Father is a God who says, '"Come now, let us reason together," says the Lord. "Though your sins are like scarlet, they shall be as white as snow; though they are red as crimson, they shall be like wool"' (Isaiah 1:18). Now that's really exciting!

O.K., that sounds good in theory. But on a Monday morning facing school/work/dole, how does it work practically? Well, God is a practical God who made people in his image. Given what I've already said as a background to guidance, what are the basic 'hows'?

Getting to grips with guidance

Just like you've got five digits on your hand to grasp things, there are five principles to help you grasp guidance. The first is simple. God won't reveal things to you if you're not living your life according to the basic guidelines he's already given you. In the Bible there are lots of guidelines laid out in black and white. Until you're aiming to live according to those, don't expect God to show you more. Notice I said 'aiming' as none of us will make the whole thing, this side of being with Jesus! An example. It's no good asking God if your boyfriend is the right one to marry if you're a Christian and he's a non-Christian. That's because God has *already* said that Christians dating non-Christians is not on (2 Corinthians 6:14). Similarly, it's no good asking God how much money to nick from your mum's purse when God's *already* said you shouldn't steal (Exodus 20:15). So the first principle is that God has already given much guidance in his word; therefore we need to know it and read it (2 Timothy 3:16–17).

Guidance in print

God will sometimes guide you in a specific way from his word by bringing to your notice verses which seem to stand out as you read them. Or you'll hear them time and again from different sources. And each time they'll seem to hammer the truth home to you. Of course, we need to be careful. It's not a matter of jab with a pin to find a verse, or you might end up with 'Judas went out and hanged himself' followed by 'Go and do likewise!' Or you might twist scripture to get what you want; like the guy who wanted to go out with a girl called Grace, and took it as guidance when he read Philippians 1:2, 'Grace to you and peace from God our Father and the Lord Jesus Christ'! But God can and will use his word, not only to show you basic guidelines, but also commands or promises for you at a specific time.

Knocking on doors

The second principle God uses to guide is that of circumstances, closed and open doors. God will often show you through apparent 'coincidences' that he wants you to go in a certain direction. For example, while looking for a job, he may open certain applications while closing others. Or he may give you enough money for a particular journey you were praying about making. This 'circumstantial guidance' can be either positive or negative.

Asking God for specific signs really comes within this principle. Gideon tried that (Judges 6) but if you set a sign for God to guide you by (a certain amount of money by a certain date, meeting a particular person unexpectedly, etc.), be sure God has said what the sign should be and not just you. You need to ask and listen, then check out the answer by praying again. Gideon made the mistake of deciding what the sign should be, without reference to God, but even then despite Gideon's weakness and lack of faith God very graciously accommodated him. I think that's because God has an amazing knack of always operating from the desires of our hearts, and not just on the amount of faith, understanding or maturity that we bring to a problem.

Sanctified common sense

The third principle is obvious. Use your common sense. God gave it to you in the first place, and will only contradict it when he needs to extend your faith, or overrule 'earthly sense' with 'kingdom sense'. What I mean by that is that occasionally God will require you to do something which may seem absolutely foolish in the eyes of other people in order to check and test whether your security and reputation are founded in Jesus or in your own ego. Or it may simply be that sometimes the apparently logical or commonsense thing to do is not what will produce the goods that have eternal fruit in the kingdom of God. Many of the temptations of Satan on Jesus in the desert were very logical and even common sense (providing bread at times of extreme hunger, creating a following throughout the kingdoms of the earth for Jesus, etc.), but the fact is that eternal fruit and the building of God's kingdom came through going God's way and not just following common sense. Remember, Satan can use common sense to try and misguide us as well as God using our common sense to guide us. An example from everyday life could be that if you're attracted to blondes, why struggle with guidance on dating brunettes? If you're naturally shy, why wrestle with guidance over becoming a full-time evangelist? Of course, God may make you less shy as time goes on, and then you may have to review the situation!

We are not alone!

Fourthly, as a Christian you must be a member of a local church (Hebrews 10:25) and should have at least one relationship with someone of the same sex with whom you can share or ask anything, and who is more mature in Jesus than you are. Someone you can trust not to be a 'yes man' but to tell you 'the truth in love'. God uses such people to guide others. Don't shop around looking for the answer you agree with, or ask too many people's advice as you'll always be given different answers, but stick with a couple of people and listen and weigh carefully all that they advise.

Fine tuning

Finally, and in one sense most importantly, there is the inner witness of the Holy Spirit (1 John 5:7). This is the real fine tuning, the hardest guidance to specify, the most dangerously subjective, but the most rewarding as we learn to hear and identify the voice of God inside us. It starts like a heightened conscience and grows as we play our spiritual 'hunches', until our hearts feel increasingly what God feels about the question of circumstance.

This is God aligning our hearts to his and our feelings to his feelings. When our relationship with him is clear and open, this most important aspect of guidance becomes the clearest. In this state we are most ready to receive guidance from a prophetic word, or a vision or picture. This guidance becomes the easiest to receive and interpret; but the hardest to act on because it requires faith, and is about walking by the spirit and not the flesh. It means acting on faith (for things not seen) sometimes in the face of fear ('Will it work out?' 'Will it happen?' 'If I jump, will he catch me?'). As we grow in maturity, so this last aspect of guidance grows within us, and we're led out by the witness of God's Holy Spirit within us. The more mature you become as a Christian, the more will God look for faith in guidance, and the less he'll spell it all out. That's because he's at pains to build our characters in Jesus; he is the Author and Perfecter of our faith. God often trusts uncertainty in guidance to the more mature, not the less, because our uncertainty and insecurity lead us back (sometimes in desperation!) to his certainty and security.

Living with the overlap

Well, those are the five principles. From doing Maths Statistics at A level (which I failed!), I remember what a Venn diagram is. It's when two or more circles overlap, and one section of each circle is included in all the others. When you're seeking God's will, and reasoning it out with him in a love relationship, look for at least three of those principles to agree and overlap. And as you grow, concentrate on the relationship side of guidance, and not just the mechanics. Remember, if you're unsure, it's not worth risking your open relationship with God over it. Then, the safest maxim is, 'If in doubt, cut it out!'

6

Tell It Like It Is

Witnessing

One of the problems of being a full-time Christian worker is that other Christians tend to imagine that things must come easier for you; that you find time to pray and study the Bible, and as for witnessing, phrases like 'it must come naturally' or 'second nature for you' float hauntingly before the eyes of most full-time Christian workers. That kind of attitude is a problem because it isn't true. Although God calls people into full-time work and therefore equips them, he calls very ordinary people. People who have some of the same problems that you and I have. Problems with praying. Or reading the Bible. Or problems with witnessing.

I was brought up in a church that fairly regularly emphasized the need to tell others about the good news of Jesus Christ. Unfortunately though, the church never specified why or how. Now knowing something is right, but not knowing why, or how to do it, generally leads to frustration, and that's what happened for me. I used to go to school and try desperately hard to compel my friends to become 'Christians' by force of intellectual argument and verbal fencing. Sometimes I'd even resort to physical force to try and make them affirm my beliefs! That's what I now realize I was doing. I needed people to affirm my beliefs. Much of my 'witnessing' came from feelings of guilt, desperation and insecurity. I reasoned that if I could make others around me believe what I believed, then *I* must be right to believe it in the first place!

So in this chapter I think it would be good to look at some very basic questions such as: 'Why bother witnessing anyway?'

You are a witness

The fact is that every single Christian, whatever his spiritual state at any given moment *is* a witness. Given that a Christian no longer belongs to himself but has been bought with a very high price (Revelation 5:9) and belongs to Jesus Christ, then every Christian is a witness to Jesus. You're either a good witness, or a bad witness. The very name Christian, which was first used of the disciples at Antioch, means 'little Christ'. We are all, like the original disciples, followers of The Way. We are witnesses who point the way to Jesus Christ. We are witnesses who testify to only what we know first hand. If we are good witnesses, then we can advise people around us not just to 'do as I say' but also to 'do as I do' (see Paul's attitude in 1 Thessalonians 1:6). Whether we like it or not, if we are Christians, we witness to him in our lives/thoughts/words. That witness will either be an accurate reflection of the love of Jesus, or it will be an inaccurate one. Good or bad, we are witnesses already.

Why bother?

But why be concerned about this witness? Why have a chapter in this book on witnessing? In 2 Kings 7:3–11 there is a superb picture of why we should be bothered with witnessing. The story concerns a city, Samaria, under siege by the King of Syria and his army. The siege had been going on for quite a while, and was very effective. So effective that donkeys' heads were being sold as food for eighty shekels of silver, and even doves' dung was considered as food! Worse still, cannibalism was being practised as children were boiled and eaten. We know that kind of desperate act can happen—

it has recently among survivors of plane crashes in remote places. And it was happening then.

Outside the city walls, kept as social outcasts and shunned by most, were the lepers. Four of them decided that they could do no worse than ask the enemy for food. After all, they could only be killed, and they were starving anyway! But on going to the enemy camp the lepers discovered that the army, due to God's supernatural intervention, had run away. So what to do? Well, at first they do what you and I would probably have done: they pig themselves on food and drink! Then they gather money and clothes for themselves. But then they stop, suddenly realizing that just a little way behind them is a city full of desperate, starving people, and that what they are now doing is selfish; it isn't right. So off they go to spread the good news. How it's received is not their responsibility; their responsibility is to tell the good news as convincingly as possible to people who need to hear.

Spiritual starvation

Now it doesn't take a theologian to see the application of this story. Whether we live in East London, or in rural northern Scotland, we are surrounded by people (friends, relatives, neighbours) who are starving spiritually. I don't think that's over-spiritualizing the picture. It's just as real and desperate a thing to starve spiritually as it is to starve physically. Both levels of hunger need to be met. Meeting one alone won't do. Whether people know it or not, or like it or not, materialism is increasingly being revealed as hollow and a sham. It cannot satisfy inner hunger or fill internal voids of meaninglessness. Many of the eighty per cent of people who in this country say they believe in God have already acknowledged that materialism alone is no answer. So have the sixty per cent of people who read their horoscopes daily. That's why so many cults have arisen and there is so much interest in the occult and fringe pseudo-sciences like acupuncture, yoga, hypnotism, transcendental meditation and the extremes of homeopathy. There is a very real spiritual hunger being felt as the famine spreads around this country, but at present much of the hunger is being assuaged by the wrong foods; foods that will ultimately harm and not feed. That's why fifty per cent of kids I talk to in schools have been to a seance, eighty per cent have played with a ouija board or tarot cards.

One beggar to another

The incredible thing is that now, as then, God will often choose the most inadequate, inappropriate people, sometimes social outcasts or misfits, to reveal real food to people. People like me. And you. Not special people, super orators, clever wordsmiths. Just people who have been at the receiving end, like the lepers were, of God's miraculous intervention in human history. People who want to share the good news of God's intervention in history through the cross of Jesus Christ.

It is Jesus whom we share with those who are starving. Jesus said of himself that he gave living water (John 4:14) and that he was the bread of life (John 6:35). The best definition of evangelism and witnessing that I have ever heard was that it's simply 'one beggar telling another beggar where to get bread'. Acts 4:13 describes how Peter and John, when they had to witness to Jesus Christ under difficult circumstances, astounded their persecutors in two ways. First, it was obvious they were ordinary, uneducated men (the Greek actually means 'ungrammatical idiots'!); secondly, the people could see that they had been with Jesus. Now that's real witness by ordinary people. And sometimes it does cost and is risky. One Greek word for witness is *martyreo* and there are no prizes for guessing what English word we get from that!

Pass it on!

The 'why' of witnessing is easily answered. If you have good news it's immoral and selfish to keep it to yourself. And since 'gospel' means God's message of good news, we should be sharing it. It's good news to be forgiven. It's good news to be guided by God. It's good news to have quality life now that goes on for ever. It's good news to receive and operate supernatural gifts for God's glory. It's good news to have God as Father, Jesus as Friend. Jesus is good news; he only ever equated himself with one thing on earth, and that was the gospel, the good news. As far as Jesus is concerned, he and the good news are one and the same thing (Mark 8:35). Let me answer the first question of 'why witness?' fairly concisely.

God's command

First, we bother with witnessing because we're commanded to. It's not an optional extra, it is part of 'Jesus' final commands to all his disciples, past, present and future. It's such a famous command it's probably even got the same title in your Bible as in mine: 'the Great Commission'. It's worth examining that commission in Matthew 28:16–20. Jesus commands his disciples to follow all that he had taught them, and to teach all that he taught them to others (that includes healing the sick, casting out demons, etc). Their aim is to make disciples not converts. All authority has been given to him, and therefore he says 'you (plural) go and you (plural) make disciples of all nations'. His authority is delegated to us. *We* are now the witnesses. Later in Acts 1:8 there is the promise of Holy Spirit power, that Jesus' disciples (that's you and me too) will be witnesses 'in Jerusalem and in all Judea and Samaria and even the remotest part of the earth' (even in Leyton where I live, or Little Wopping-in-the-Marsh or wherever you live!). Note that witnessing is something you *are* ('*be* witnesses') not something you just *do*.

Next, we bother with witnessing because of compassion. In Mark's gospel chapter 5 Jesus got a boat, went across the lake, got out of the boat and delivered one man from demon-possession, and then went all the way back. (Read it for yourself: he did all that for just one man.) The same Jesus taught about one lost sheep being worth the effort of searching even though ninety-nine were accounted for (Luke 15:4–7). This same Jesus cried over Jerusalem with great compassion (Matthew 23:37). The shortest verse in the whole Bible is 'Jesus wept' (John 11:35). At the tomb side of Lazarus, Jesus was so greatly moved with compassion that the original Greek says he snorted convulsively as a horse would with distress (John 11:38). Compassion is a godly emotion, sympathy isn't. Sympathy commiserates with the problem and identifies with it; compassion identifies with it and is mingled with positive action. If I'm starving I need someone with an Indian takeaway, not someone to sympathize!

You can't work this kind of compassion up. It's no good my asking you when you last wept over Little Wopping-in-the-Marsh, or when I last wept over Waltham Forest. Just like the loaves and fishes, you give to Jesus what little you've got, and he blesses it and increases it. But he asks you to be involved in the distribution. So ask God to produce that compassion in you for people on the tube trains, on buses, on the streets, aimlessly rushing from one event or experience to the next, with death the only certainty in their life. These are *your* neighbours. Friends at school. Workmates. Mum and Dad. Brothers and sisters.

God's constraint

Third, the command and compassion of Jesus made Paul feel constrained to bother witnessing, so I guess we should too. We should have a kind of compulsion to tell 'in season and out of season' whether we feel like it or not. There's an effete kind of Christianity exemplified in some streams of the church that waits until God says, 'Witness now!' Here's news; God always says, 'Witness now!' You can't mature as a Christian without witnessing; it's part of maturity. You can't put your house in order before you do it; it won't be in order unless you're witnessing. Like Paul, you and I should aim to be compelled to witness (2 Corinthians 5:14).

God's consequences

Lastly, why bother witnessing? Because finally at the end of our life there are the consequences. It's unpopular but very scriptural. On the occasions when I've had to directly confront the works of the enemy as he's possessed human lives, I've been faced with the hideous reality of the consequences of hell. God sends no one to hell, but many decide for themselves, in rejecting Jesus, to go there. These consequences are for real. They break God's heart. It's the cost of free will and the price paid for the right to love; the cost is wrong choice and the right to hate. That means my relatives, my friends, face the enduring consequences of their choice. If I can influence them for good I will. I don't want to scare anyone into God's kingdom, because he is a God of love, but I'd rather people accepted him for the wrong reasons, than rejected him altogether. Revelation 20:15 makes the consequences clear. I don't want to hear anyone say about me, 'But Pete, you never told me!' I don't want anyone to face those consequences. Neither does God. The onus to be a witness to life is on us.

That's why we bother.

Who's responsible for results?

But if it's our responsibility to witness, are we responsible for the results? I know lots of Christians, young people especially, who take the burden of results off God and onto themselves.

I never converted anybody. Neither did you. Only God through the Holy Spirit can bring about conviction leading to repentance, with the co-operation of the individual! So your responsibility is to tell, not to collect scalps, or notches on your Bible! Not to be involved in gangster evangelism, but in friendship evangelism. Of course, if you're faithful, God will also make you fruitful, but that's his responsibility, not yours. We share and we persuade (2 Corinthians 5:11) just as you'd persuade someone to leave a burning building, if you thought anything about them! Don't be blasé ('Oh well, I've shared the gospel, now it's down to them,' or, 'I shouted it from a soapbox in the High Street but the sinners wouldn't listen') but equally don't be condemned by the enemy ('You're no good, they didn't listen, you needn't bother witnessing any more.').

Whose territory?

Before we look at how we can effectively share our faith with friends, let's just look quickly at the area of 'whose territory'. Witnessing is spiritual warfare, and as such must be surrounded by prayer if it's to be effective. Witnessing will also therefore inevitably involve you in 'kickback' or attack, but you're protected from that on Jesus' winning side. What do you expect in a war anyway? I've just discovered that our work in north-east London is being actively prayed against by a local spiritualist church. Non-Christians are blinded (2 Corinthians 4:4) and in order to plunder Satan's territory we need first in prayer together to bind him and make him helpless (Matthew 12:29). Under *Jesus'* authority. But let's be clear on territory; I don't want anyone caught out for trespassing!

God created

This world is God's world because he created it (Genesis 1:31). In creation it was a very good world with man in God's image at its apex. God has never taken his hands off the world. He is totally and integrally involved in it (Colossians 1:17); that's theism. Deism imagines a creator who has left the universe to run down uncontrolled like a clockwork toy, no longer interested or involved in it.

Satan corrupted

The Bible, in balance, also teaches that this is Satan's world, because he corrupted it (Genesis 3; 2 Corinthians 4:4). Satan is a counterfeiter (even of the gifts of the Holy Spirit) but he can never be a creator. For every good gift of God Satan attempts a counterfeit corruption. God gives us sex so Satan pushes lust. Satan perverts God's gift of food by encouraging gluttony. Beauty he corrupts by turning it into vanity. And so on.

Jesus conquered

But it's never an equal balance of power between God and Satan, a kind of cosmic seesaw. The Bible teaches that it's *Jesus' world* because *he conquered it* (John 12:31; Colossians 2:15). It's *your* world because it's Christ's (Ephesians 2:6). We are heralds not apologizers.

How Jesus witnessed

How do we witness best to the goodness and grace and the life and love of Jesus? Since in Scripture Jesus is always the best possible example, it might be a good idea to look at how he handled witnessing.

In John 4 there's a classic example. Read through from verses 1–42 and I'll pick out just a few of the lessons you and I can learn from this. First of all, in verses 4–6 there's the principle of 'God appointments'! Verse 4 says Jesus had to go through Samaria—but geographically he didn't, if you look at a map. Has the Bible got it wrong then? No, Jesus *had* to go through Samaria because he had an engagement booked with one woman by a well. Normally Jesus would have gone round Samaria, not through it. This 'God appointment' booked by his Father wasn't terribly 'convenient' geographically speaking, although it was to be very important and productive. Jesus was weary. Not just tired. Weary. And it was very hot out in the open, at noon. And he was alone, not surrounded by friends. But it was God's timing, nonetheless, to present an opportunity of witnessing.

God appointments

If you want to witness but don't know how, start by booking a 'God appointment'. Of course, you'll need to take it when he gives it to you. He won't force you. But if you say tomorrow morning, 'God, give me today an appointment where I can share something of you in a natural way to someone, something that'll stretch me but I can cope with,' then I guarantee he'll book the appointment! Sometimes just being there as the presence of God is enough as a starter. A recent experiment in New York City, USA, took priests out on the street with a New York Police patrol, and just the presence of the people of God had a calming, practical effect on the rate of crime incidence.

You'll be obliged

Moving on in John 4, there's a very practical principle demonstrated by Jesus as to how to witness to your faith in him. That's found in verse 7 where Jesus asks the woman for help before he gives help to her. Simply, he places himself under obligation to her. It's obvious; I get most easily irritated by people who have all the answers before I've even asked the questions. Being an escapologist I know a bit about locks and keys. I found it irritating when recently buying a set of security padlocks for one of my stage escapes to have the locksmith tell me all about the locks and what I could and couldn't do with them. Of course, to be honest, it was partly my pride that was affronted. But also, if the locksmith had listened to my ideas first, I'd have listened to him better! As it was, all he did was to succeed in getting right up my nose!

And that's how Jesus responds here to the woman at the well. *He* asks *her* for a drink of water. Something she can do for him, before he offers Life to her. If you put yourself under obligation to the person you're witnessing to, you've earned the right, by receiving, to give back to them. So in schools, I encourage the kids to tell me about their favourite music or football team, or TV programme, and I listen to them. That earns me the right then to tell them about news far better and more exciting than West Ham's recent game, or *Minder* on TV or U2's last concert. Jesus isn't instantly defensive or condemning with this woman. He begins where she's at, and communicates with her, and receives from her before giving to her.

Crossing barriers

Another interesting point here. In verse 9 the woman is amazed that Jesus has spoken to her because (a) he's crossed social barriers because she's a woman and Eastern men don't speak to women outside, and (b) he's crossed religious barriers (and geographical barriers) because he, a Jew, is talking with a Samaritan. The Samaritans were a mixed race resulting from the intermarrying of the Israelites left after the fall of Samaria with people from other nations who introduced idol worship into the Jewish religion. So the Jews hated the Samaritans and vice versa. What's our lesson? We too need to break down the social, religious and geographical barriers that tend to push us only towards certain kinds of people. You know what I mean. The British reserve means that if you smile at someone on the Tube in London and they're female, then you're trying to flirt with them; if they're male, then it means you're homosexual! It is the same reserve that stops you talking with your neighbour. If you're in the sixth form, it stops you talking with a fourth year. If you're a bank clerk, it stops you talking with the manager or the window cleaner of the bank. We need to cross these false barriers of prejudice, ignorance and fear, just as Jesus did here.

Prompting questions

Note next in verse 10 that once Jesus has got the woman into conversation, he doesn't hammer her with the whole counsel of God in one go! Instead, he drops into the conversation an interesting, provoking and stimulating comment that almost demands further response from the woman. We've lost the impact of it through familiarity, but Jesus says the equivalent of my meeting you in Sainsbury's and offering you a can of living baked beans! It provokes reaction. I know in a lesson in school that I have only to say, 'I was talking to God the other day...', and I get a reaction before I can finish the sentence. 'What do you mean, talking to God, did you hear his voice then? How does he talk back to you?' etc. Odd comments carefully dropped into the conversation, or even unfamiliar lapel badges (fish symbols etc.), will provoke reaction that can be an 'in' for your witnessing. The woman didn't cotton on to what Jesus was saying at first; she wanted living, eternal water just so that she wouldn't have to keep going to the well! Your first point or comment doesn't need to convey the whole plan of salvation instantly. Better if it leads on to further conversation, as it does here in John.

The Communist cells in the United States of America operate on a similar principle. They preach commitment to the Communist cause to their members, then send them out onto the streets to speak out and propagate the message of Communism with their neighbours. Of course, being ill trained they meet all sorts of problems, so at the next cell meeting they're given more teaching on techniques and then sent out again. And so on, progressively. It's a simple principle of giving enough to leave people wanting/needing more.

From the general to the specific conviction

But it doesn't stay general, does it? Jesus doesn't allow the conversation to remain vague or impersonal. By verse 16 the Holy Spirit is homing in on a point of specific conviction, and that's the next important point of witnessing I want to make. Providing it is the Holy Spirit who's convicting a person of sin, and not me or you being self-righteous or condemning, we mustn't shy away from specific sin; it's no good metaphorically patting someone on the head when they start to get uncomfortable under the conviction of specific sin and saying, 'Well, never mind, don't feel too bad, we're none of us perfect, it'll all pan out O.K.' There is a need, as Jesus does, to be direct and straight with people. Much of society (and especially young people) is looking for definitive answers, rights and wrongs, absolutes. Much of society has denied them that. We as God's people mustn't. It's no good denying what the Holy Spirit is doing through the work of conviction. It is, after all, one of his jobs (John 16:8).

Gifts witness to Jesus

Jesus is here operating a specific gift of the Holy Spirit: the gift of knowledge. When we witness we need to ask for and operate specific Holy Spirit gifts, particularly perhaps gifts of wisdom, knowledge, and discernment—they save so much time in witnessing (and in counselling)! I reckon that's why we have two ears and only one mouth; we should listen twice as much as we speak, and we should listen to God with one ear, and the person with the other ear! So in verse 16 Jesus puts his finger right on the 'sore spot' of sin in this woman's life in a way that he couldn't possibly have known humanly. And that leads us right on to a classic response—the red herring syndrome!

Fishing for red herrings

I can't read verse 19 without imagining the woman going red and stuttering her way through the sentence, 'Ah, yes! Well, er, I can see that you're…er…a prophet. Yes! A prophet, that's it! Now…some people say this, and some people say that, blah, blah. Er…What do you think?' It's classic. As the Holy Spirit convicts, we wriggle. The woman is hauling in a red herring to escape from the point. And we must be prepared for, and even encouraged by such red herrings. There are a limited number (about seven) of them that come up time and again, and at the end of this chapter we'll look at the most frequent ones. Just for now, though, some ground rules from Jesus' example in verses 22–24.

Catching red herrings

He doesn't say, 'Now look here, you stupid woman, that's quite beside the point, so let's get back down to where the truth really hurts, shall we?' No, very gently but firmly Jesus answers her question and then he applies the important principle of 'refocus'. In other words Jesus gets the woman off the red herring ('Where do we worship?') and back to the personal issues ('It's not where you worship, it's who you worship'). Gentle firmness is the key here, as in 1 Peter 3:8–17.

Refocusing on Jesus

Now the best way to refocus that I've come up with is to keep your thoughts focused on Jesus in the first place. If you go into a witnessing situation, train your mind to think 'Jesus... Jesus...Jesus....' Then the conversation won't drift from its personal application of Jesus into a kind of woolly, pseudo-intellectual sea where red herrings abound!

It's easily demonstrable that our minds are capable of this kind of focusing/refocusing. Two years ago, when I knew my old Cortina had had it, and I was about to get a Simca to replace it, I suddenly found that the number of Simcas on the road had dramatically increased! They were everywhere! Of course, the numbers hadn't really gone up, but my mind was ticking over 'Simca...Simca...Simca...' so I noticed them more. And so with Jesus. When you're witnessing, keep Jesus in the front of your mind, and avoiding red herrings gently but firmly won't be so difficult.

Demonstration of the gospel

The last pointer I'd like to emphasize from John 4 comes in verse 26. At the end of the day our lifestyle must demonstrate the gospel, including the power of God through gifts, signs and wonders. People need to see as well as hear about the gospel. The world is weary of words only. A words-only-gospel is not the true gospel, which throughout the New Testament comes to people in power with deeds, signs and wonders (1 Thessalonians 1:5; Romans 15:19). That's another reason why we should be asking God for greater gifts and more power—so that we can *show* as well as tell the gospel of Jesus Christ and the kingdom of God. The Old Testament prophets demonstrated God's word (Isaiah 20; Jeremiah 13; 19; Ezekiel 4; 5; Hosea 1; 2) and so did Jesus (John 1:14; Acts 1:1).

Proclamation of the gospel

We also need the proclamation of the gospel. John's gospel is partly about seven great signs and demonstrations of the kingdom and seven great proclamations of Jesus as the gospel, the great 'I am'. And John 4:26 is one of these dramatic statements. If it wasn't true that Jesus is the Son of God, then what he states in verse 26 would be blasphemy, because the phrase '*I* (who speak to you) am (he)' actually embodies the name that Yahweh had given to himself in Exodus 3:14: 'I am that I am.' Jesus is in effect stating that he is on a par with God. In John's gospel it's most clearly stated in John 8:58, 'Before Abraham was born, I am.' The same statement causes the crowd to react in horror as they tried to stone Jesus. At some stage in our witnessing there has to be some clear proclamation of who Jesus is, what his claims are upon us, and what our response to those claims is.

So there we have some very practical principles that Jesus used in his witnessing. And we should use them too. In the closing pages of this chapter I'd like just to outline some of those recurring red herrings and suggest how to answer and refocus your questioner.

Roasting old chestnuts!

In one sense there are no definitive answers to these questions, otherwise they'd have ceased to be the hoary old chestnuts that so many of them still are. If you'd like to do more detailed reading on this kind of issue, then I'd recommend Paul E. Little's books *Know What You Believe* and *Know Why You Believe*. Michael Green's *You Must Be Joking*, J. N. Anderson's *Evidence for the Resurrection*, Frank Morrison's *Who Moved the Stone?* and Josh McDowell's *More Than a Carpenter*, *Evidence That Demands a Verdict* and *More Evidence That Demands a Verdict* are also useful.

Now, those questions. From my experience in classrooms and on London streets, the most common questions occur in the following order of frequency:

1. Who made God?
2. What about suffering then?
3. Why should I believe in God if I can't see him?
4. What about Adam and Eve?
5. Isn't the Bible a lot of old fairy tales, and doesn't it contradict itself and hasn't it been added to?
6. Isn't it all just in the mind, a kind of mental crutch?
7. How can you possibly believe in miracles?

The best way to answer such questions is (a) to be gentle and firm (b) to refocus on the person's relationship to Jesus (c) to be biblical in your answer and use references (d) to be visual/pictorial in your answer (visual aids and stories aid the memory and the understanding) and (e) to be personal in your answer—you always communicate who you are from your spirit, not what you believe from your head. So use *your* experience; you are unique and God's appointment *will* match you.

Just to show you the kind of thing I mean, here's a sample of how I might answer those seven questions.

1. Who made God?

The idea is that if God made everything, then where did he come from? Well, for a start, the Bible says God isn't physical, he's spiritual. It's only physical things that have to obey physical laws, for example every piece of matter has to have a beginning, a decay period (or lifetime) and an end. That's a problem with the Big Bang theory; where did the gases come from to cause the big bang in the first place? But God isn't physical (John 4:24). He never had a beginning and he'll never die. Since time is measured by change and Jesus Christ, along with God, is the same yesterday, today and for ever (Hebrews 13:8), then time doesn't restrict God—he made it, and although he constantly operates within it, God himself is not subject to the passing of time. Otherwise you end up with the ridiculous situation of a God made earlier on by an older, bigger God, who in turn was made even earlier by an even older, bigger God! Either God is without beginning and end, or by definition he isn't God.

2. What about suffering?

Or famine/wars/earthquakes/handicapped babies, etc? It's vital to point out that suffering cost God his Son Jesus Christ (John 3:16). He's not detached from suffering and he doesn't cause suffering. In fact whenever possible God heals the suffering. But this universe is now in decay. Scientists call it entropy. We call it the fall. Caused by the sin of people like you and me, the whole creation is spoiled (Romans 8:19–22), although God created and intended it good and perfect (Genesis 1:4, 10, 12, 18, 21, 25, 31). If you tried to run your personal Hi-Fi off the mains without an adaptor, ignoring the instructions, you'd expect it to go wrong, and you'd be responsible for the result, not the manufacturers. So with God. We ignore him and his instructions for living, and then blame him when it all goes wrong! Even so, God loves us so much that he still gets involved in the breakdown, even to the extent of losing his Son. And although it breaks his heart (even more than yours) he has to allow suffering to continue, because it's the cost of having a free will—the right to choose wrong (and its consequences) rather than to choose right (and its consequences). Who'd be left if God decided to wipe out all evil and every cause of suffering at noon today? Not you. Not me. Instead, God keeps on identifying himself with our suffering, waiting as long as possible so that as many as possible will turn to him (2 Peter 3:9). The amount of world suffering is a reflection of the patience of God's love, not the hardness of his heart or his inability to do better. World suffering reflects *our* sin and evil, not God's.

3. Why should I believe in a God I can't see?

The ultimate answer to this question is that you're saved through faith (Ephesians 2:8) and that faith is 'to be sure of the things we hope for, to be certain of the things we cannot see' (Hebrews 11:1). But that's not so tough! We all believe in lots of things we can't see. For example, who would deliberately stick their fingers into a plug socket? But we can't see electricity. Who'd be foolish enough to say they weren't surrounded by hundreds of different voices floating unheard through the air? We believe in radio waves, don't we? Or microwaves in our ovens? Or the wind? How many people deny the existence of love? Or hatred? Or embarrassment? They're very real, but you can't see them. Yes, you *can* see the effects of them. The lights go on at the flick of an electric switch. The radio comes to life when it receives the radio transmission. The chicken gets cooked in the microwave oven. The trees bend in the wind. You fall in love. You hate that person and snub them. You go red with embarrassment.

It's the same with God. You can't see/hear/touch/smell/taste him, but you can see the effects of God. On nature, on circumstances, on other people. In yourself. Personal testimony that combats coincidence by the frequency of God's intervention in your life is vital here. And the reason friendship is based ultimately on faith is because God longs for a depth of relationship that combats mere 'seen' circumstances and is based on trust and unreserved commitment through love. If, at the end of the day, I could scientifically prove God, I wouldn't worship him. He has to be bigger than me, beyond my total understanding, or else he wouldn't be God. Though the evidence of the order within creation, people's complexities and sins, archaeology and history all indicate the reality of an unseen God, finite minds reaching out to the infinite God still need faith, otherwise our God would be too small!

4. But how about Adam and Eve then?

The idea is that you can't trust the statement that God actually made everything in six days, when science has 'proved' we evolved over millions of years from fish and monkeys. This is a massive issue, and I'm certainly not scientifically qualified enough to argue it out in depth. Enough to say that if God is God there's no hassle in him doing things exactly as recorded in Genesis 1–3. Science has only posited a theory of evolution that is scientifically incapable of being proved through deductive, analytical, scientific reasoning, because it's non-repeatable!

Biblical truth isn't ultimately at risk, even if evolution were to be a fact, as there are legitimately defined ways of interpreting scripture other than literally (e.g. parables, poetry, visions). Science at best can tell us how things happen, but never 'Why'. The mechanics may be scientifically explained, but the reasons cannot. There's no conflict. The God of the Bible is also the God of science, and while he is bigger than both, he will never contradict the former, though he may the latter. Genesis 1–3 isn't primarily about how, it's about why. This is how you can refocus your questioner. Genesis 1–3 is about why God created everything—in order to have a love relationship with people like you and me. It's not a textbook on how. It doesn't say how. What's important about Adam and Eve is that God made them, loved them, and they fouled it all up. Genesis is all about separation from God as the result of disobedience, sin and pride and God's inability to look on sin despite his desire to rescue sinners. And so back to Jesus!

5. Isn't the Bible just a load of fairy tales?

Part of the answer to this question is covered in the chapter on Bible study and reading. The Bible is an incredible document, spanning thousands of years both in the writing and telling. Despite a variety of authors, it's cohesively linked by a progressive theme—God's intervention in human history. Archaeological, historical, documentary evidence all support the remarkable accuracy of the recorded events of the Bible. Eyewitness accounts preclude the idea of the Bible being 'added to' by fanciful disciples at the time of writing. You could not write about the sinlessness of Jesus and his resurrection to people who were around at the time...unless, of course, the story were true!

As for adding to the original material over the centuries, two things mitigate against that. First, the Jewish tradition was of handing on stories *word for word* very accurately until they reached a scribe. Secondly, the Bible was complete by about 70 AD and therefore within eyewitness account times, so there would have been no time for these 'phantom' additions to occur.

Most people asking this question haven't even read the Bible. They can't point to the so-called 'contradictions' (for example, where Old Testament law like an 'eye for eye, tooth for tooth' in Deuteronomy 19:21 has been replaced—not contradicted—by New Testament grace like 'love your enemies' in Matthew 5:44; or where lists are incomplete, such as omitting mention of Cain's wife in Genesis 4, or having different ordering for different emphases, such as the order of creation in Genesis 1 and 2 where two accounts differ, but are not mutually exclusive, such as are found in the gospel accounts of the empty tomb at the resurrection of Jesus.) These 'contradictions' all need to be considered in the light of the fact that the Bible is one hundred per cent accurate in what it says about people, their thoughts, actions and motives, and in what it says about God. Look at what it says, for example, about itself in 2 Timothy 3:16. The Bible ought to have a Government Health Warning affixed to it:

'Danger, reading this book can change your life!'

6. Isn't it all in the mind?

A psychological crutch? Wasn't Jesus just a good man? Here's where your list of answered prayers comes in handy. How many answered prayers is your questioner prepared to write off as 'merely coincidence'? Or how many times God has healed you or others? If it's all in the mind, how come it works exactly as though there is an external God? And anyway, if I was making up a God in my mind subconsciously, I'd make his rules a good deal easier to keep and more comfortable than ones like 'love your enemies' or 'no sex outside of marriage'! Try asking your questioner what he or she leans on—we all lean on something. Friends, Mum and Dad, boyfriend/girlfriend. Or sex, drugs, fashion, money. I know who I'd prefer to lean on! And he wasn't just a good man. How can a good man go round telling blatant lies like 'I and the Father are one' (John 10:30)? Jesus was either a liar, or he was mad—a lunatic who really believed what he said but was unbalanced. Or he's who he said he is; the Lord. There's no evidence he was a lunatic—psychologists studying the gospels reckon Jesus Christ was the most well-balanced person who has ever lived. There's no evidence he was a liar—the nature of his personality and teaching doesn't fit with his being a con-man. He can't have been merely a man, because of what he claimed. The alternative—he is Lord.

7. But you surely can't believe in miracles, can you?

Why not? If God is God I'd expect him to be able to do miracles. What's the virgin birth to God? Or water into wine? If he's God he can do it. You may not believe in God, but your thinking is back to front if you say, 'There can't be miracles, therefore there's no God.' You might say, 'There's no God, therefore there can't be miracles.' But then you've got to find another reason why there's no God.

Anyway, miracles do still happen today. I've witnessed

them. Share something of what you've witnessed when this question arises—I think we all need to see God's kingdom as well as talk about it. Seeing *and* doing is, after all, scriptural (James 2:20, 26, etc.).

Let me finish the chapter by saying that there are a limited number of things that will hinder you in witnessing. First, sin will stop you because your heart will condemn you—you know you are wilfully not living what you're sharing. (Remember none of us do one hundred per cent.) This conviction of sin makes you ashamed of the gospel, and you need to repent and start again (1 John 1:9; Hebrews 10:22).

Wrong teaching will stop you. Teaching such as: 'Wait until God tells you to share your faith.' He *has* told you. Or, 'Only a few (Billy Graham, Luis Palau, Eric Delve) are evangelists.' This is true though it's estimated by church growth experts that ten per cent of any congregation who are Christians will have the specific ministry of an evangelist, and that doesn't just mean preaching to crowds from a platform, but also equipping the body for service (Ephesians 4:11–13) and talking with school/workmates, etc. We're not all evangelists; we *are* all witnesses.

Apathy will hinder your witness. Ask God for his perspective on people—seeing their potential, not just their problems—and ask for his heartbeat of love and power for the lost. Don't rely just on your love.

Finally, fear of people will stop you. Don't let it. It's a trap. Rather, trust God and his perfect love for you to overcome fear of what people think. Your security can be in Jesus, not your peer group. Equally don't be afraid of your witness doing harm rather than good; that's God's responsibility (Isaiah 55:10–11). And if, like I used to be, you end up after all this being scared of people wanting to become Christians because you don't know what to do, here's a little formula to use. It's mechanical whereas new birth into the kingdom of God never is, but at least it's a framework for the Holy Spirit to fill and take apart should he wish to. Why not learn it now?

The 'mechanics' of conversion

Admit—that you can't make it, and that you are a sinner (Romans 3:23; Romans 6:23).

Believe—that Jesus died for you personally, the perfect Son of God, to win you back to God, and that he's risen, alive, and the Boss (1 Peter 3:18; John 3:16).

Count—the cost of discipleship, not conversion; it's *all* you have and are (Mark 8:34–38).

Decide—to act on the three above statements and surrender to Jesus as King and Saviour (John 1:12).

Receive—the new life, forgiveness and the fulness and power of God's Holy Spirit, including his gifts and fruit (Luke 11:13).

That's enough to get me and you started and moving. How about it?

7

Under the Thumb

Peer Group Pressure

Ask most young people to describe a typical Christian, and you'd get a very revealing answer. As I visit schools, challenging non-Christians about Jesus, there emerges a very clear stereotype of what a Christian is, what he does, what he looks like. The stereotype can come from a variety of sources such as a kind of folklore based on tradition, or a media portrayal based on your Benny Hill/Dick Emery Vicar impersonations, or even worse, it may be based on actual observed examples. The hardest barriers to overcome are those that we, the church, have erected. Barriers of traditionalism and bad communication within a church which is seen to be irrelevant to modern society's needs and questions.

The Christian stereotype is of a pretty boring, wet, sombre 'black-suit, black-look, black-book' person, lacking in any sense of adventure with little or no sense of humour, politically a Conservative and a conservative dresser who dislikes modern music and fashion. There are still peer group pressures within some Christian circles to actively promote and encourage this stereotype into reality. As though such externals, based retrospectively on some nostalgic 'those were the days' mentality of the times before the permissive sixties, were the way to true spirituality!

A dangerous snare

Peer group pressure is a very dangerous snare. Let's just define our terms. Peer group pressure occurs when you are moulded/persuaded/threatened to conform to the standards of your peer group of friends or colleagues. The group you most want to be 'in' with dictates the nature of your behaviour, fashion trends, choice of music, attitude to life, way of thinking etc. There's a limited sense of security in peer group pressure because people are, by nature, gregarious. There's a kind of herd instinct in us, basically because God created us to live together in a family. The trouble with this limited security is that group pressure security is a type that eventually stifles you—it surrounds and binds you from the outside, instead of liberating you on the inside. Even when peer group pressure is aiming to produce positive results (for example, a well-integrated young people's fellowship), it is of itself a bad thing. You and I have to be free to decide for ourselves, to think through and live out issues of faith, behaviour, personality and dependence on God for ourselves. When this individual freedom is exercised, and it can only be exercised through the freedom that Jesus brings (see Romans 6:16–18 and John 8:31–36), then we can work on relating to others without fear of being pressed into something we're not. That's why Romans 12 starts off by warning of the dangers of peer group pressure, being conformed, oppressed and moulded into the world's pattern. It then goes on to tell you how to avoid the influence of peer group pressure, how to relate to other people in serving them but not being pressed by them. God wants you the way you are. Yes, he'll change you where those areas of thinking, behaviour, personality have gone wrong or are lacking.

But he changes you 'from glory into glory'! He doesn't depersonalize you into a kind of evangelical production-line model! Being changed to be like Jesus doesn't mean we all end up the same. It means we become more really ourselves. Our true selves. The way God always wanted us to be with the attributes, gifts and character qualities of Jesus, but also with our own individual personalities. From the hairs on your head to your fingerprints you are unique, made in God's image, and that's the way he'll keep you. Your name is written in Jesus' book of life. Jesus is currently preparing a mansion in heaven for you. You shouldn't try to be someone else's man or woman. But you can be Jesus' man, Jesus' woman, by being transformed.

That's how to avoid peer group pressure. You need to be transformed, changed radically and integrally. Not conformed to what everyone else thinks/says/does/feels. And transformation comes through the renewing/remaking/refilling of your mind. The way you think about yourself. About others. About God.

Acceptance at any price?

The main reason that peer group pressure is so formidable is that we fear man more than we fear God. We want acceptance desperately, but we tend to want it from man more than from God, which is stupid, because at best man's acceptance is temporal and it's always conditional, whereas God's acceptance is unequivocal; God loves you as you are. This desire for acceptance is especially true of adolescents. They need to be accepted, part of the group, an 'O.K. person'. They need that security and the sense of belonging. And many sell themselves to achieve it, only to find it was a hollow, temporary 'belonging'.

Being yourself in Jesus

When you get a sense in your heart as well as your head that God loves you, accepts you, then here is freedom and security. You don't need to conform with others then, you can be yourself in Jesus. Graham Kendrick put it really well in a song he wrote a few years ago.

> Being myself is not half so bad as I thought that it might be
> Living in the love of Jesus who loves the likes of me

And isn't it good to know that I don't even have to try
To fight for a place in this old human race
Since I'm already home and dry....

So I'm being myself in Jesus
And He's being Himself in me
I'm being myself in Jesus
And that's the way to be
I'm being myself in Jesus
And He's being Himself in me
And the life that He gives is the life that I live
And I'm living it naturally....

How many times I've tried to be something that I'm really not
Thinking so much of the things I lack
I forget the things I've got
Yet it's so hard to take when the image comes tumbling down
But God gives you grace when you're put in your place
Down on your face on the ground....

If I should say what I really feel well would you laugh at me?
And if I should show my weaknesses, would you walk all over
me?
And if you should find the real me, well tell me would you turn
me down?
Please tell me no, to keep my confidence growing
In this family love I've found.

So I'm being myself in Jesus
And He's being Himself in me
I'm being myself in Jesus
And that's the way to be
I'm being myself in Jesus
And He's being Himself in me
And the life that He gives is the life that I live
And I'm living it naturally.

Blowing up or growing up?

Take the image of a balloon, blown up and tied. When pressure comes on the outside, it changes shape; it conforms to the external pressure and changes shape. A bit like the way our behaviour can change depending on whether we're at school, with our mates, or at YPF with our youth leaders! Or at work in the canteen, compared with our sainted mask at church! When enough pressure is applied to that balloon from different directions, it eventually gives way under pressure and...BANG!!...it's gone. That can be equally true of your life. There are warnings of this same pressure in the Bible (Proverbs 29:25; Mark 4:16–17; Ephesians 4:14–15; James 1:6–8).

What that balloon needs is a kind of inner stability, something on the inside that will fill it out and cause it to be the shape, even under pressure, that it was designed to be. That transformation is what you and I need. That's being filled with the Holy Spirit.

Pressure point

O.K. Supposing you're aiming for that kind of transformation. What implications does all this have for the Christian young person, when it comes to fashion, music, drinking, swearing, racialism, finances, etc?

First, let's get the negatives out of the way. It means you don't need to hide behind an image. You don't need to project a particular exterior that isn't really you. You already have an image—God's. And that's what you need to project. Images based on particular modes of dress or music seen in discos, wine bars, trendy youth clubs, etc. are all out to (a) impress others (b) effect membership of an 'in' group (c) exclude others, usually in an attitude of superiority (d) find an identity, or more usually, falsely create an identity, which in reality is a show or mask.

You don't need this. There's nothing wrong with wanting to belong, to be liked and appreciated. But when that desire *dictates* to you how to live, behave, dress, spend your money in a way contrary to God's best, then you're in trouble (see 1 Corinthians 6:12 and 1 Corinthians 10:23). Don't adopt an image—*be you*!

Will the 'real you' please stand up!

Actually discovering who you are is far more exciting than trying to be someone else, or hiding the real you behind camouflage. But supposing the real you actually likes streaking your hair with pink, or wearing earrings as a bloke, or dressing in Oxfam suits, or Robert Klein track suits or Pierre Cardin jumpers! Supposing you honestly (and you have to be ruthlessly honest with yourself, as a Christian, about your motivations) like those fashions, and don't wear them merely to be acceptable, to keep up with your mates, to project an image, or to rebel against your school or parents? Well, if so, then great! Go ahead and be yourself. There is no Christian ideal concerning dress sense, or hair styles, and no amount of quoting Old Testament references about not shaving your head (Leviticus 19:27; Numbers 6:5) will convince me otherwise. Those particular Old Testament references and rules were cultural and not spiritual principles. We mustn't quote Scripture to reinforce our own predetermined prejudices. It seems clear to me that the weight of Scripture indicates that God is concerned with the heart, not with externals (1 Samuel 16:7). That's what much of 1 Corinthians 8 and Romans 14 is about; have a read!

Keeping an eye on principles

The principles to watch when it comes to fashion are a) that your motivation isn't dictated by peer group pressure (belonging to the crowd, presenting an image, keeping up with your mates); b) that you're not rebelling against your parents or authority placed over you. The Bible is clear that you have to obey your parents, even if you disagree and even if they're wrong (Colossians 3:20; Ephesians 6:1). It's equally clear that you and I are to be subject to other authority (see Romans 13); c) you need to be a wise and responsible steward of money. We can't always do everything we'd like to, even when what we'd like is good. You need to decide in the light of your income and your giving money to God's work whether you can/should pay £20 for a LaCrosse pullover, or £60 for a pair of crocodile leather mocassins, or whatever. Is that good stewardship at this time and place? Has God said 'go ahead' or am I prompted by desire and greed? Within these constraints I think God has given you a free hand. There's nothing wrong with being fashionable providing you're not sucked into the fashion-world mug's scene where your wardrobe of clothes is out of date every year, and you find yourself manipulated into constantly striving, at considerable expense, to keep up with make-up, clothes, hair fashions. Most fashions are manufactured by the design houses just to part you from your money. Don't be anyone's mug. It's good to be fashionable, but I'd rather be an unfashionable fool for Jesus than an up-to-date mug for Gallini!

Just a quick word on the current trend, among males and females for 'sexless' fashion. Girls deliberately trying to look like blokes, or more commonly, males deliberately dressing like girls (for example, Boy George, Marilyn, Divine, etc.) is expressly forbidden as a principle of creation (see Deuteronomy 22:5) not of culture. It's a confusion or even denial of the God-given attributes and characteristics of male and female. And for you as a Christian, it's out.

More pressure points

Peer group pressure extends beyond fashion, of course. It's not just those pressures that make people try to be individuals by (strangely) making them all look alike! Peer group pressure can be more insidious, less obvious, than all of that. It affects where you go and with whom. It entices you to go into pubs and discotheques under age. It prompts you to spend too much money and to drink as much and use the same dingy vocabulary as those around you. Don't. You'll lose out. You'll stop being God's person, and start being someone else's. Keep a watch on your behaviour and attitudes. Don't change, chameleonlike, to blend with your background. Have the guts, conviction, determination, and the transformation of your mind through the Holy Spirit, to stand out and be Jesus wherever you are. In any case people will more likely respect you for that than for being a chameleon. And if you can't cope in certain situations, don't go there. Don't mix with those people. The risk isn't worth taking.

You and your music

Towards the start of this chapter I mentioned music. This is another area of pressure and controversy, and it's very hard to be objective because we all have our likes and dislikes. It seems to me that the wider your tastes are the better, because by not liking certain types of music (or food or whatever it is) then you're the loser—you don't gain anything by not liking things, whereas you do gain if you appreciate a wide variety of experiences. Unless, of course, those experiences or music are actually harmful, bad, evil. In that case, by disliking evil, you stand to gain righteousness.

A recent book in the Christian subculture, which needs no further publicity from me, took a very hard and decisively negative line on 'pop' music and its use in evangelism. It needs to be said that there is legitimate concern over the music we expose ourselves to as Christians, but we mustn't overreact in an immature or fearful manner—that brings us as great a potential for bondage as does the excesses of the music scene itself.

I think these concerns exist, not because there's anything inherently evil in particular forms of music or beats (for example, rock or Reggae beat with all the connotations of 'African tribal worship' and 'Voodoo Drums'), but rather because of the underlying spirit and message of the music. The music, its form and beat are, I believe, a neutral carrier; what matters is the content or 'feel' that's poured into this carrier. There's nothing more spiritual about a Hebraic than about a Rock rhythm; it's the message you convey that counts.

For that reason, I believe that much of the anarchic, violently aggressive content of rock and roll, and similarly a lot of the immoral schmaltz of country and western music, is harmful to your walk with God. Philippians 4:8 conveys it well; it can't be good to expose yourself deliberately to negative influences. And these negative influences aren't restricted to just those two types of music.

Similarly, an increasing number of groups are actively pursuing not just anti-Christian communication. Many pursue anti-Christian lifestyles, but that alone needn't stop us appreciating their art form. Whatever is good is of God, not Satan (see James 1:17). It's a mistake to revere the artist as well as the art just as it's equally limiting to reject the art because of the artist. Where there is actual devil worship and satanism that *must* be avoided at whatever cost to your social life, your bedroom posters, or your record collection. Such groups include Black Sabbath, AC/DC, Iron Maiden, Alice Cooper, etc. Again, the safest and best maxim to follow here is: 'If in doubt, leave it out!'

So within these parameters your musical taste is your own, under God. Not other people's. Why not go over your preferences in your mind and ask God for wisdom and discernment? Anyone with an ounce of discernment should be able to receive the promptings of God's Holy Spirit over such groups and record sleeves as 'Bat out of Hell' by Meat Loaf. There are some tracks played on National Radio that I find myself wanting to turn off till they've finished. I may not know why directly, except that something about them disturbs my spirit. So I do turn them off. Sometimes I may be overreacting or imagining it, though if I've asked for wisdom and discernment then I play my 'spiritual hunch' and trust God for it. But even if I'm wrong, I'd rather not risk it. The constant check is: 'Would Jesus be happy with me listening to this?'

Pressure to be racist?

I'd like to finish this chapter by looking at one other area where it's easy to stray into the conformity of the world, and that's the subject of racialism. I live in a fascinating area of north-east London. Fascinating because in the north of our Borough it's a very middle-class, white-collar commuter-belt, and that's reflected in the churches and schools. In the middle of the Borough it's average working-class London, and in the south of the Borough it's rather run-down, East-end London with high unemployment, large black population and third generation 'immigrants' (who are every bit as British as me). Interestingly the part of our Borough where racialism is most rife is in the north, where there are far fewer West Indians, Asians etc. That's the area where the National Front has its stronghold. Here ignorance of lifestyle and not actually knowing people who are all too easily the subject and butt of uninformed bigotry and prejudice, all combine in racial hatred and discrimination, and sometimes violence.

There is tremendous, sometimes overt, sometimes covert, pressure from various peer groups (school mates, work mates, social strata, even church groups) to conform to a world view of racialism which sees those different from you in race as inferior. Or less intellectual. Or morally lax. Or more inclined to criminal activities. Or unreliable in timing. Yet many never explore either the unfounded prejudice that such attitudes are based on, or investigate the occasional valid social reason for their fears/feelings/attitudes. (For example, some cultures do view things differently, some employers/police do discriminate against blacks.)

Two-way prejudice

But racial prejudice works both ways. It has nothing to do really with who is in the ethnic minority/majority, or whether there should be positive discrimination in favour of blacks. It's really to do with heart attitudes. Racial prejudice is born out of fear, ignorance, selfishness, pride and the desire for domination. It runs contrary to all of Jesus' teachings on 'love your neighbour' (Matthew 5:43) and his attitude to races as revealed in Luke 10:30–37 and John 4:4–45. It has no part in the standard of love that Jesus has set for us and enabled us through the Holy Spirit to live out (1 Corinthians 13; Galatians 5:22–23). It has no part in the kingdom of God. The early Christian church had to stand firm against attempts to manipulate people culturally and racially (see Acts 10, 11, 15; Galatians 3:28). These New Testament attitudes are attributes of our God, who earlier in the Old Testament had laid down very clear laws and responsibilities in the Pentateuch for his people Israel's treatment of the 'sojourner' or foreign visitor in their land. (See Exodus 22:21 Leviticus 19:18, 33–34; Deuteronomy 1:16; 24:17; 27:19.)

You and I have to raise our eyes from the merely social factors to God's word, and we also have to understand that our enemy, the devil, is strategizing to separate, divide, wound, and promote tension, discord and hatred. According to the Bible, it was a direct result of sin and pride and the Fall that the nations split in the first place (Genesis 11:1–9).

God's models for unity

These things apply as much to blacks' attitude to whites as whites' attitude to blacks. I've occasionally met vehement, embittered black church leaders who, having been hurt in the past by white Christians (for which there is no excuse), will now make few if any moves towards reconciliation. Reconciliation between races has to be a two-way action; as a recent Greater London Council poster said about racialism—'If you're not part of the answer, you're part of the problem.' Whether you're white or coloured, racialism should remain a non-starter, a dead issue. It should be irrelevant, both in our lives and therefore in our churches, and therefore potentially in our society. I understand the advantages of having so-called indigenous congregations (that is, all-Asian churches, or all-West-Indian, etc.) but I remain very unconvinced that that is a scriptural model.

Jesus established his church at a time and in a place rife with racialism and oppression, and one of the church's unique features was the blending of people and backgrounds (racial and social) in harmony and love, as Jesus taught. So it's no good pleading that culturally the church today is faced with different prospects on this issue of racialism. Integration is a scriptural model, and as such it is both practical and workable. I've seen it work locally and I've seen it around the country. The Elim Church in London, Kensington Temple, currently has the largest number of nationalities in membership in any one church in the UK. Working, learning and worshipping together there is a combination of 200 plus nationalities! If it can work in London, scene of many racial riots, it can work elsewhere, too, through the Holy Spirit and our determination.

The pressure's off!

So when it comes to any kind of peer group pressure, be free to be a servant of the Lord Jesus Christ. Not bound to be a slave of your peers and therefore, ultimately, of Satan. Jesus came to make you your own person, so that you could take all you are, and give it to him, in love and obedience. The life *he* gives is real life, and freedom. I'll swop peer group pressure for God's pressure any time! How about you?

8

Getting to Know You

Personal Relationships

It wasn't the ideal situation. I tried my best to look concerned and to concentrate on what this teenage girl was saying, but it wasn't easy. When the four of us had begun to chat together the weather had been fine; sunny, a bit blustery perhaps. But now, as we listened to the girl's story—her hatred of being 'expected' to be a Christian by her Christian parents—the weather had broken. There we were, sitting in one corner of a big canvas marquee on a Christian holiday camp site with a mini hurricane howling around us! Not only could I hardly hear the girl, but feeling slightly damp I looked down to discover that I was standing in a stream of rain water pouring under the tent wall and out under the table we were grouped around! Definitely not ideal!

Apart from the damp surroundings that situation runs like a video replay through my experience of counselling young people. In fact, it runs through my own experience of growing up in a Christian family too. I'm profoundly grateful *now* for the Christian upbringing I had—the truths I was taught, the example I experienced, the things I was shielded from. But at the time 'family relationships' sometimes meant a series of hassles to go through.

God's sinless grandchild

First I thought I was one of God's sinless grandchildren. You know the kind of thing I mean; everyone else is a sinner, you can see it just by looking at them, but you are not. You're pretty decent, really. You were brought up the right way. You lived a life of sin and degradation before being gloriously converted at the age of only three-and-a-half! In fact, you never really did much wrong. Never got the chance! You understood about and believed in sin; in others. But as for you; your parents were Christians. My grandfather was a Methodist minister. So you must be a Christian—a kind of 'grandchild of God'.

The only trouble is God doesn't have grandchildren! Only sons and daughters. That was my first hassle. I never had a 'conversion' experience because I'd always believed it. And that used to worry me sick! Had I been merely brainwashed? Was I really a Christian? Why have I no 'second birthday'? It wasn't until University when I had a very real encounter with God, through the filling of his Holy Spirit, that that particular fear was allayed. Suddenly *I* was a sinner; God was real and personal.

Great expectations

Next hassle. Living up to Christian parents' expectation, or going your own way? Did I want to find God for myself, or try and make a go of it without him? For a year at University it was touch and go. Don't misunderstand me—I didn't get into the drugs/drink scene, or wild orgies! I did go to church every Sunday. I was very *self*-righteous, but not very *God*-righteous. It was my life with God tagged on, instead of God's life with me tagged on. So in my second year at University God had to start to take me apart, bit by bit, showing me (a) who I really was (b) who he really is and (c) that the two could come together through his love.

Pride before a fall

Third hassle. The new, enlightened, whiter-than-white Pete
goes home during vacations to preach dogmatically, vehem-
ently and all-too-often gracelessly at Mum and Dad! He
realizes he has to learn humility, patience, respect for wisdom
and experience, etc. He's still learning! It's an often repeated
pattern—it's my pattern.

The aim for the enemy

But it's not the only pattern. Maybe reading this chapter
you're thinking, 'I wish I had the chance of that problem.
Mum and Dad aren't Christians at all. They laugh at me.
Stop me going to YPF. Encourage me to drink/smoke/sleep
around.' Or maybe you're thinking, 'I don't have a Dad/
Mum,' or even, 'My Dad isn't safe to be left with. He hits me
or he molests me.' It's no good pretending these strains in
family relationships don't happen. They do. You only have
to counsel young people to see the horrific potential of wrong
family relationships. Let's face it, all our personal relationships are prone to failure, and I know of few areas that Satan
takes more delight in trying to destroy than our relationships
with families and friends. So what are some of the ground
rules for you as a young person? In one chapter we can't
cover all the ground, but a lot of it comes back to basics.
Usually you won't be responsible for the actions of your
mother/father/brother/sister/boyfriend/girlfriend, but you
will be responsible for your reactions. Let's look at family
relationships first, because the body of Jesus Christ on earth,
the Church, is likened to a family. Other Christians are your
brothers and sisters. What's the scriptural model for relationships?

Easy to say, hard to live

Good family relationships are marked by (a) forgiveness—
see 1 John 4:20–21; (b) counting others better than yourself—see Philippians 2:3; (c) preferring others—see Romans
12:10; (d) submitting to one another—see Ephesians 5:21;
(e) bearing one another's burdens—see Galatians 6:2; (f)
loving one another—see 1 Corinthians 13:4–8.

So the obstacles to good family relationships are (a) grudges
and bitterness; (b) conceit; (c) selfishness; (d) rebellion and
pride; (e) independence; (f) hardheartedness. The contrast is
obvious. The bridge between the two is confession, repentance, accepting forgiveness and being cleansed (1 John 1:9).
That bridge is through Jesus Christ and the power of the
Holy Spirit, not your effort. You don't have it in you to
change yourself—remember all those broken New Year's
resolutions (Galatians 3:2–3)? You co-operate and build the
mould; God fills you. You 'put off the old and put on the new'
(Ephesians 4:22–24; Colossians 3:9–10).

Improve your serve!

And do it practically! We all need a change of heart and
attitude if we are to become the servants that Jesus wants us
to be. Jesus himself declared a number of times that he didn't
come to be served but to serve and that those who wished to
be great in his kingdom would have to learn to be the
servants of all. Such references are scattered through
Matthew's gospel, for example. Everybody in this world is a
servant or slave in one form or another. If you are not a
Christian then you are a slave to sin (see John 8). You serve
either God or his enemy, Satan. But in order to have the kind
of servant heart that Jesus wants we need to have heart
surgery to change our attitudes to make us more in line with
Philippians 2 and Jesus' own example. Helping with the
ironing or hoovering wouldn't go amiss in most households
on a practical level, and would probably go down better than
a sermon! Similarly cleaning, gardening or washing the car,

spending at least one evening each week at home with your parents isn't a bad idea either. In these ways you serve with your time and your presence. Watching your timing, coming in when you're told (even if it's 'unreasonable') and when you go out informing your parents where and when, for how long and with whom, are also good' ideas. Appreciating meals won't go amiss. And how about, if your parents don't do it, actually initiating family Bible study and/or prayer times—hard work but worth while! This kind of practical serving can be applied not just to your home life but also to the time that you spend at school. Consider your attitude to authority set over you (Romans 13), the way that you do your school work or your job for that matter (Colossians 3) or the way you share your experience with those at school or at work who are younger than you. It's marked how in many school Christian Unions there's no communication between sixth formers and fourth formers and in the kingdom of God such attitudes are definitely out.

Ground rules for relating

The principles for relating apply to the natural family as much as to the church family. They're difficult to live out in either, but hardest perhaps at home, where you're seen at your worst and not just your most spiritual! At home you're known for who you are, not who you'd like to be. The ground rules for parent/child relationships are simple. You may say they're impossible. I'd say they're only impossible if you want them to be impossible. But if you *want* to live them out God's way then they cease to be impossible, through Jesus Christ alone (Philippians 4:13). They are to be found in Exodus 20:12; Ephesians 6:1–4; Colossians 3:20–21. Here are your commands to honour your parents and increase your own lifespan! Here are straight commands to obey your parents! No cop-outs like: 'I'd obey them if they were Christians.' Yes, your first obedience is to God, but the clear statement in balance is found in Colossians 3:20—'Children, obey your parents in everything, for this pleases the Lord.'

Problems with pride

I'll say right now that your main enemy will be pride. 'I want to make my own decisions.' 'If I go God's way, it'll look as though I'm submitting to my parents, and I don't want it to look like that!' But listen. Sometimes your parents may act unfairly, unwisely or defensively, but nearly always they will act out of right motives. They'll want the best for you. They'll act from the motive of love. Like you, they're human. They may think they're wiser and more experienced, but like you they too will make mistakes. Like you they may not always see that or admit it. For this reason humility, tolerance, forgiveness and patience become key factors. On both sides. Parents and children.

Let go and let grow

It's hard for parents to let go and let grow. Previously you always needed them, and now you don't so much. It's difficult for Mums and Dads to watch their children make mistakes, yet you need the room to make mistakes in order to grow. And it's difficult for you to get a proper perspective on it: to admit that you don't have all the answers, that 'experience' does count for something and isn't always patronizing, that your parents probably do care an awful lot. It's give and take; you both need room to adjust. You need less room to adjust than you think; they need more room to adjust than they think.

Worth working at

That's enough about families to be going on with. But do remember it's important to work at these relationships in families because God ordained the family; it's his institution, and we owe it to him to let him make it work for us. It's also important because the family mirrors the church. Because of that fact your attitude in family relationships will affect your attitude to God and his church. For example, a bad relationship with your earthly dad could give you a bad view of God as your heavenly, perfect Dad. Inability or lack of desire to get on with or forgive your blood brother or sister can affect your attitude towards Christian brothers and sisters. It's important to work at letting God get it right in us. If you have particular bad memories or attitudes towards members of your family which are deeper rooted in you than just your unwillingness to get them sorted out and work at them, (and you must be honest in this) then it may be that you need to receive ministry from the person in your life with whom you have a close spiritual relationship. We have already talked about the need for everyone in the Christian family to have both a 'Paul' and a 'Timothy'.

Sex

Another very tricky area in personal relationships is the whole scene of boy/girl relationships. Sexuality is one of the strongest motivating factors that you ever experience, whether you're male or female, heterosexual or homosexual. The stimuli and responses may be different, but the drive is the same and as powerful. You'd expect that biologically as the sexual drive is integral for the preservation and procreation of the human species. But, of course, sex is not merely a biological necessity. The most vital sex organ of your whole body is...wait for it!...your mind. God created sex and sexuality, not Playboy magazine, and he made it fun! Your sexuality reflects part of God's image (Genesis 1:27). If you're a bloke, you can be really glad and affirm that God made you male. If you're a girl, you can celebrate your femininity. You don't need Women's Lib to set you free as a woman. Jesus has already done that in his own attitude to women in his own society and for all time. You've got God's Lib. Both sexual identities are in the Godhead; the imagery of God is as both Father (Romans 8:15) and Mother (Isaiah 66:12–14). One is not better than the other. The roles are different and that's expressed not only physically (in case you hadn't noticed!), but also in terms of stress factors, emotional responses, even spiritually. (For example, many women are more 'intuitively' aware of God's guidance than men.) We have to beware of the *world's* sexual stereotypes (for example, men don't cry, women are bad drivers, men wire plugs, women make meals, etc.) Sexuality is part of God's very good creation (Genesis 1:28, 31), but sexuality is also subject to the fall.

Guidelines for good

When it comes to 'going out' with someone of the opposite sex, what are our guidelines? Well, I hope the chapter on guidance might help here. I do not believe, for example, that there's only one girl/boy in the whole world for you, and needle-like you have to hone in on them in the haystack of the world. Nor do I believe that you must end up marrying the first girl you date! Though I do think that when you're actually 'going out' with a girl/boy, you should at least consider marriage as viable. Not that you plan for it, but that you can imagine it as possible as far as you can tell at that stage of the relationship. Otherwise you're probably going out with your partner for selfish reasons and someone is going to end up hurt. As my mum used to say—'It'll end in tears!' Social dating is fine, of course, though it is worth noting that girls tend to find platonic friendships more difficult to handle than boys as they become more easily involved emotionally.

I think God gives us very definite ground rules in guiding a boy/girlfriend relationship and then says, 'Now, let's work it out together within that framework.' And there's the crunch. What *is* the framework?

Unequal yoking

Well, first off, a Christian dating a non-Christian is out. That's clear from 1 Corinthians 15:33 and 2 Corinthians 6:14 where the reason is stated. We all know stories that are exceptions ('eventually she converted him'), but that's a testimony to God's grace, love, forgiveness and patience. It's a 'despite' not 'because of'. The fact is that for every story that ends happily, there are five more Christians going out with non-Christians who eventually lose touch with their God. If your greatest love and security is in Jesus Christ how *can* you share the deepest love of your life with someone who doesn't even believe in him? The answer is that you can't. That's unequal yoking. It'll drag you away from God through the conflict of interests it involves. And it'll also lay you open to greater sexual temptation. I'm afraid that all the old illustrations of 'one rotten apple in a barrel full of good ones turning the barrel full of good ones bad' are all true here. Unequal yoking for a Christian is out.

A place and a time

Second ground rule. Sexual intercourse is a beautiful gift, the ultimate act of self-giving and unity between two people. It operates at every level: physical, mental, emotional and spiritual. It's God-created, God-given. He is no prude! But neither is he a fool. God knows that every spiritual experience is either in one kingdom or the other. It's either of light or darkness. Of good or evil. Of God or of Satan. And God has determined the limit within which this particular spiritual experience (sexual union) takes place—namely within marriage, and *nowhere else*. Within marriage sex should be good and enjoyable because it is of God. Outside marriage it can be physically good (though often it isn't, due to guilt, mistrust etc.) and even emotionally good (though often it isn't, due to insecurity, selfishness etc.) but it can *never* be spiritually good. Sex outside marriage is still a spiritual experience, but now it's of Satan. Therefore it carries enormous potential for hurt—to yourself, others, and God.

Obvious risks

The physical risks are obvious. Last year 170,000 abortions were carried out in the UK. The incidence of venereal disease (gonorrhoea, syphilis, herpes, AIDS, etc.) is rapidly on the increase. Cervical cancer occurs more in those indulging in early sex. Bad side effects of the most popular form of contraceptive, the Pill, are particularly observable in young girls. Less obvious but just as real are the emotional traumas of abortions, guilt, split families—the legacies of hurried gropings in the back seats of cars, or fumbled lusts in darkened bedrooms. If the scene sounds tawdry and dirty to you, it's because it is, though God *never* intended it to be that way. A fire in a grate is beautiful but a fire on a living room carpet is disastrous! Sex in the right context, marriage, is fantastic. Outside of that, it's not only dangerous, it's forbidden.

The least obvious risk is the spiritual, but it's *very* real. Sexual activity outside God's limits produces spiritual bondage—you give legal territory to Satan over an important part of your life. You may become gripped with lust and obsessed with sex. You may feel guilty but helpless, become unable to pray and your relationship with God (and then others) takes a nosedive. Satan has a field day because you've left the door open to him. And *never* think that Satan will ignore an open door—he won't. Don't think that for you it's O.K. 'Well, we're engaged, so it's all right,' or, 'I love her anyway,' or, 'It feels so good it *must* be right.' God has said it isn't ever right outside of marriage. If you don't believe my warnings on its consequences, have a look at the following references: Matthew 15:19; John 8:41; Romans 13:13; 1 Corinthians 6:18; 1 Corinthians 7:9; Galatians 5:19; Ephesians 5:3; Colossians 3:5; 1 Thessalonians 4:3; 2 Timothy 2:22; Revelation 21:8.

Let's be clear about one more definition; fornication is the same thing as sex outside marriage. Fornication or sex outside marriage is sexual immorality, along with other sexual sins as, for example, homosexuality and adultery for which there are also specific biblical references.

How far can I go?

Lots of young people then say, 'Well, how far can I go then?'
I'm really not in the business of defining the outer limits of
sexual experience that stop just short of sinning. If you're
asking that question, then you're asking the wrong question.
It betrays your heart's desire to sin, or as near as possible,
and get away with it! I understand why (I'm a red-blooded
bloke too, you know!) because of the strength of sexual
desire, and *that's not wrong*. It's natural to be attracted *sexually*
to a member of the opposite sex, natural, good and right. Just
as it is to enjoy food. But gluttony is wrong. Get your *motives*
right in your heart, and then you'll start to find the right
limits. A few guidelines....

Why not explore how far you can go in a positive area of
friendship with your boy/girlfriend? What interests (other
than sex!) do you have in common? Consider areas of agree-
ment and disagreement. How well do you chat together? Do
you pray together and have Bible discussion and worship
times together? Do you mix well with other Christians and
non-Christians together? Do you lead one another deeper
into God? Are you good friends? How good are you at considering the best for your boy/girlfriend? What motivates
you when you kiss him/her? What do you get out of it? Or
what do you give? Is your motive in embracing one another
to offer love and affection, or only to arouse you sexually?
Whenever your *motive* is sexual arousal outside marriage,
then you are on tricky ground. Do you pray together before
going out to a disco or party? Would Jesus be embarrassed in
your company when the two of you are together alone?

Practical hints

We have to be very honest with ourselves and each other
when we consider questions like these, because our hearts
can be deceitfully wicked (Matthew 15:19). There are lots of
practical hints, like not frequenting rooms with beds in when
there's just the two of you! Not having *long* sessions alone, or

kissing/cuddling marathons! Blokes should be particularly aware that your sexual arousal is quicker than your girl-friend's, so *you* be especially careful; a girl responds quicker to a smile than to a fumbled grope. Girls should therefore be diplomatic about the kind of clothes you wear. (Summer can be very difficult for blokes!) Remember that petting is part of foreplay, and that both petting and foreplay have only one logical goal and that's sexual intercourse. So all three are out, outside of marriage. Don't be exclusive in your relationship; being with others, developing friendship, prayer and Bible reading together will all help. But ultimately it's your heart's desire that dictates your action! Do you *want* sin or not? Making rules can help. I could say that caressing under the clothes your boy/girlfriend is wearing is out, but such rules are limited. I've seen (and experienced) sensual caressing, which is just as deliberately sexually stimulating on the outside of clothes, as I've seen fumbled gropings underneath clothes that are a total 'turn-off'. You have to be honest with yourself and each other—you have to get your hearts right. Have a look and read at Psalm 51 together maybe.

A giver or a taker?

It might be appropriate just to spend a little time at this point in the chapter looking at a subject that's not strictly 'personal relationships', but that crops up again and again when talk-ing about personal relationships with young people, and that's masturbation. The Bible is perhaps strangely, certainly providentially, silent on this whole matter. Yet for *many* Christians, particularly Christian lads, it's a real problem.

Masturbation is a complicated way of describing the act of sexually arousing yourself, usually to the point of climax. It's far more prevalent amongst blokes than girls. Estimates indicate that ninety per cent of all males have masturbated at some time in their lives over an extended period of time. The figure for girls is forty per cent—much less but still signifi-cant. Masturbation can range from simple sexual self-relief to an obsessive and furtive practice. Almost always, even with the non-Christian, it carries the stigma of ridicule and guilt.

For the Christian, masturbation can actually become the criterion on which failure in the Christian life is built—constant temptation followed by constant defeat is the story of *many* Christian young people in this area of life. Putting it simply, that's ridiculous!

God's priorities

The reason masturbation isn't discussed in the Bible is not because it's unimportant. (And *don't* quote Genesis 38:9 at me, because that's a totally different matter to do with motivation, intercourse and contraception.) By that argument you could say that abortion (also not *explicitly* mentioned) is not important either—which it certainly is. But let's get one thing clear straightaway. To you reading this it may seem that masturbation is *clearly* the biggest hurdle and sin in your life, cutting you off from God and stunting spiritual growth. But I *guarantee* you that to God it doesn't appear that way. While you may put masturbation at the top of the list of things in your life to be sorted out, I very much doubt that God does. To him your anger is a higher priority, or your bitterness against your sister, or your fear of his Holy Spirit. So let's shed a little light and perspective on the subject. If you masturbate and find guilt a problem, remember that it's 'normal' (I didn't say *right*). Ninety per cent of other blokes and forty per cent of other girls do too. God views the problem as minor not major, *and* there *are* answers. Working from that, you're not beaten before you begin.

Conviction not condemnation

If masturbation *doesn't* cause you hassles with guilt, then I'd say two things. You're very rare. And don't let this chapter make you feel guilty. As you grow in God he'll let you know by the Holy Spirit if you're doing wrong. Remember it's the Holy Spirit who convicts and Satan who condemns: Romans

8:1 is true even when we feel it's not.

My own feeling, both from personal experience and talking with many other young people, is that masturbation *is* usually harmful in our walk with God, and therefore best avoided.

At best masturbation confuses the roles of giver and receiver—sexual gratification is meant to be given by you and received by another, and given by another (of the opposite sex) and received by you (all within the context of marriage). At worst masturbation is self-centred. You're most prone to masturbate when you feel lonely or insecure as an attempt to find love or security, which can only truly be found in Jesus Christ and friendship with others.

I'm quite certain that much of the feeling of guilt associated with masturbation (a sense of elation, urgency, of wilful disobedience, followed by the plummeting sense of failure *yet again*) comes from condemnation, not from conviction. God knows our weaknesses, Jesus Christ was himself a man, without sin, but tempted in every way (Hebrews 4:15). Condemnation cripples, conviction changes. You can be sure that if you're about to stop trying to resist this temptation, or jack in your faith because you've failed again, then you've listened to Satan and not God's Holy Spirit. The Holy Spirit says quite simply, 'O.K. you failed again. Are you sorry at this moment? Will you try *again* with my help? Then pick yourself up, don't feel sorry for yourself, don't try to earn forgiveness. You *are* forgiven. You are clean again.'

Just another temptation

Beating this temptation is no different from beating any other—look at the chapter on temptation again. Reckon yourself dead to sin. Replace the temptation not by fighting it but by focusing on Jesus Christ. That includes prayer, fasting, worship and praise, Bible meditation. It includes co-operating with God very practically. When you're first tempted, go to be with people. Do something practical and absorbing *at the time*. Pick up your Bible. In the chapter on Bible reading I mentioned the advantage (particularly for blokes) of reading a couple of verses last thing at night and first thing in the morning—two prime times for masturbation to be a problem. *Avoid* situations which you know arouse you sexually and tempt you to masturbate. And remember the difference between temptation and sin—it's not sin to become physically aroused, but it is sin to cater to that arousal, or deliberately prompt it. I know of very few people who've claimed to me that they are able to masturbate without fantasy in their thought-life becoming lust; that *is* sin (Matthew 5:28). Telling someone of the same sex who's older in Jesus than you are will also be a help. They can then pray for you. You may need someone to pray with and for you if this is a real problem—it helps keep things in perspective. You may simply need to receive ministry so as not to be bound by the problem.

'Wet dreams' or 'nocturnal emissions' as they are impressively called, fall into a different category. Again the vast majority of males experience these sometime or other—they're a natural means of sexual relief over which you have no conscious control, since they occur during your sleep. You need feel no sense of guilt over these dreams at all, and although you have no control over your subconscious mind, the good news is that God can have. He knows when you sit down and get up and lie down (Psalm 139:1–4) and you can commit your sleep and dreams to him; I think you'll be surprised at how effective God is at coping with your subconscious (Psalm 4:8). Again, late night/early morning Bible meditation is a great help here.

Homosexuality—God's view

In the closing paragraphs of this chapter on personal relationships I'd like to look, albeit briefly, at the subject of homosexuality. That is, the sexual attraction that can exist between two members of the same sex, male or female. (Female homosexuality tends to be called lesbianism.) In the space I have to devote to the issue, I have little chance to cover other than what I see as the basic spiritual principles.

If this is *your* problem and situation, please forgive this brevity. It's not because I want to gloss over the issue, or that I view it as of little consequence—no bald statement of fact or even biblical truths can do justice to the love, understanding, acceptance and concern that this problem merits.

Having said that, and in the face of the proliferation of 'Christian' gay church movements, I do think we need some clear scriptural understanding. There is *every* biblical evidence that homosexuality is a sin. (Check the references for yourself: Romans 1:26–27; 1 Corinthians 6:9–10; Leviticus 18:22; Genesis 19; Judges 19:22; 1 Timothy 1:10.) Despite occasional (*very*) rare chromosome X and Y deficiencies, which can produce *physical* gender confusion (though not necessarily *emotional* identity crises), there is no medical evidence to indicate that homosexuality is a disease, although it may certainly be a learned environmental tendency. There are indications of environmental influence (for example, dominant and possessive mothers, weak or even absent fathers), but no one is ever merely a *victim* of sin, and the Bible makes it clear that homosexuality *is* a sin. As with every sin, there comes at least once in a person's life the choice of going God's way or their own. So no one is ever a victim of homosexuality. Moral choices are available to everyone. It is modern society which substitutes the word 'disease' for 'sin' in a wide range of issues from sexuality to stealing. Environment *may* predispose a person towards the tendency of same-gender sexual attraction, but the sin of homosexuality lies not in the tendency (which is temptation) but in the act (which is sin). We should always aim to avoid temptation (Matthew 6:13), but we should wilfully reject committing sin.

A sin among sins

Please note that homosexuality is *a* sin, not *the* sin. It does come under the stern category of warnings in Romans 1:21–32 and 1 Corinthians 6:18, but then so does heterosexual sin, for example sex outside marriage. Homosexuality is a sin because, although it can be based on genuine love, it goes outside the limits which God imposes on male/male and female/female love into the realm of sexual attraction and expression. God has said that sexual expression should be limited to marriage only, and marriage to male/female only. Homosexual 'love' denies the duality of sexual identity and role which exists within the Godhead and in whose image you and I, male and female, were created. Like everything created good by God, love and sexual love (*agape* and *eros* in the Greek) are capable of being corrupted by Satan. Homosexual 'love' is one such corruption of God's created intention.

Sinners—God's view

As with all sin God hates the sin, but loves the sinner. The homosexual is *not* an object of ridicule, pity or loathing. He or she is a person with thoughts and feelings. He or she has the same call on God's grace for forgiveness and cleansing as you and I have. No more is asked of the homosexual than of the heterosexual; avoid temptation and abstain from sex outside its proper context. The heterosexual has the potential of sexual fulfilment within marriage. The homosexual has the potential of establishing sexual *security* and identity initially with Jesus' understanding, love and acceptance, and ultimately with Jesus' power to change. He does not, however, have the potential for sexual fulfilment as a homosexual. Not all homosexuals do become heterosexuals, just as not all married men stop being tempted by women other than their wives. The alternative to homosexuality can be fulfilment in sexual *identity* (not sexual activity) and security in Christ's love and forgiveness. But it can also be radical change in sex orientation.

God's alternative to sin

I'm not going to attempt in one part of one chapter to say how that's possible except to say that, allowing for occasional, definite, dramatic breakthroughs of God's Holy Spirit in counselling situations, bringing deliverance, forgiveness and healing is usually a long-term struggle. Habits and thought patterns have to be unlearned and renewed. Battles have to be won. Ministry from others usually must be received. You can't and shouldn't try to go it alone. Share the fear. Share the guilt and the failures. But be real and honest with yourself, God and others. Remember that a feature of practising homosexuals is sometimes a compulsion to deceive or lie. Remember that sexual confusion during adolescence is 'normal' if not natural. Most adolescents go through a 'homosexual' phase during puberty. Don't carry scars of guilt/fear/worry from any such past phase or activity.

Judgement starts with the family of God

The Christian church has much to answer for in its negative response to homosexuals, both Christians and non-Christians. Failure to condemn the sin and forgive the sinner has resulted in confusion, bitterness, and unbiblical denominational conferences and reports. Fear of the unknown, or fear even of what may be our weakness, keeps us at a distance from the people with real problems. That's not good enough. If this is your problem, then please forgive your brothers and sisters who in the past have reacted wrongly. But more importantly, as with all personal relationships, please forgive yourself, let God forgive you, and having started to get it sorted, go on in God.

9

Me and My Shadow

Self Image

I have already mentioned that self identity and self appreciation are vital elements of a well-balanced Christian life. During the course of this chapter I'd like to investigate why they are vital. I spent too many years living the Christian life without a sense of self acceptance and I'd like to help you avoid that particular trap.

Why be a worm?

I hope in the course of this book you'll pick out the unscriptural nature of what I call 'worm theology'. God knows what we're like through and through, and he doesn't need reminding that left to our own devices we are sinful and far from him. That's why he had to love us *first*. Having loved you first, God has now put a price on you in the face of all creation (including his enemies)—the price of his Son Jesus. So your evaluation of yourself no longer counts, because you no longer belong to yourself. It's not your evaluation that counts; it's God's.

You are unique. You are a prince. Or a princess. You're in the middle of God's kingdom. You're clothed in Jesus' own robes of righteousness. You've been given a new heart, sprinkled clean by the blood of Jesus Christ (Hebrews 10:19–

22). It doesn't count how you view yourself, though God can change that. It doesn't matter how others have viewed you, though God can alter that for his reputation's sake. What matters is what Almighty God himself has said about you.

Just as in nature God has created every single snowflake and cobweb to be completely different in pattern and design, so he's created you as unique. You are a very individual channel for his goodness and power to flow through. From your fingertips to your brain patterns, from your personal DNA structure to your personality, you are unique, and uniquely God's creation.

The need to learn to love

Unless you learn to accept yourself as God sees you, there will be all kinds of implications that will stifle your growth, and maybe even your desire to grow in Jesus. Self identity and self worth are particularly important to a teenager, who is in any case struggling with the questions of 'Who am I?', 'How do others see me?', 'Am I acceptable/attractive?', 'What do people say/think about me when I'm not there?' Find your answer in Jesus, and you've really found an answer that'll last (John 8:31–32).

What are some of the effects of not having a good self image? Well, it's obvious that you and I can't love other people the way we should, unless we have God's love in us. When we feel how God feels for others, then we can start to love and accept others as they are, without thought for race, background, class distinction, appearance, etc. But we can't feel how God feels for others unless we've first had it revealed to us how he feels about us. Otherwise all we're talking is theory. It's only second hand if we haven't felt God's heartbeat of love for us. Imagine how much he loved Jesus. Remember those times, perhaps in worship, perhaps alone in your room, when you felt almost overwhelmed by your love for Jesus. (And I do hope you have.) If that's what you feel for Jesus, imagine what he feels for you. Our love is imperfect, but his isn't. Jesus loves you. With everything that the Creator God has in him, he loves you.

Unless you've felt that love for yourself, you can't properly feel and express God's love for others. That's the first implication of having an unhealthy self image.

Neither can you possibly love God properly unless you're prepared to learn to love yourself. By undervaluing yourself, you directly accept a lie from Satan, cast in the face of Jesus who died because he valued you as precious in God's sight. You end up making God a liar, and the words of Jesus lies. If you hate yourself, how can you fully love a God who loves you enough to let his Son die for you? You're contradicting such a great God, so great a way of salvation.

And if you don't accept yourself with all your faults, as God does, then you'll find it very difficult to accept others with all their faults too. You'll become trapped in the lie of this world that performance equals worth and you'll set such high standards for yourself and for others that it's impossible to meet them. Perfectionism is easily sin. Performance does not equal worth. Worth is God's estimate on a person.

There are further effects of not loving yourself. If you love yourself, then you'll find it easier to let others love you too. If you accept yourself as a 'suitable receptacle' for people to invest love and attention in, then you'll find it easier to invest love and attention in others. And if others are similarly learning to love themselves, then you'll find it easier to love them because they'll be finding it easier to receive your love. (That may take reading through again!) Love God. Love yourself and be loved. Be loved and love others.

Lack of self acceptance can cause problems in other areas of your life too. Looking for love, acceptance and comfort, yet unable to accept it even when it is given, can confuse you over whether you're a giver or receiver of love and comfort, and that can lead to many problems. Self hatred can lead to subconscious self punishment through undereating, and in extreme cases to anorexia nervosa, or to overeating, or excess drinking, or drug abuse, or sexual experimentation. In 1985 fifty per cent of the world's population were under the age of twenty-two. As you read this book, over the next thirty minutes, twenty-nine children will attempt suicide; fifty-seven young people will run away from home; fourteen teenage girls will give birth to illegitimate babies; twenty-two girls under the age of nineteen will have received an abortion; 685 teenagers will take some form of narcotics which they are already regularly taking; 188 young people will experience a serious drinking problem; 286 children will become victims of broken homes; and a further 228 children will be beaten, molested or otherwise abused by their parents. A survey revealed that seventy-nine per cent of parents thought that they communicated well with their children, but that eighty-one per cent of the same children said that their parents were not communicating with them at all well. It's unlikely that many of these young people at present love themselves, or as a result of these and other areas of sin and stress will love themselves in the future. (Figures relate to the UK).

The unfulfilled need for self worth can drive you to seek a people-centred job. To try and ease the empty feeling inside you, you take a job where you know you're needed. More than a few people go into full-time Christian work from such insecure drives. The trouble is, it doesn't work. You end up needing to be needed, which leads you to encourage people to have an unhelpful reliance on you until you become so involved that you are no longer capable of offering the objective help and perspective they need to solve their problems. The truth is you need their problem because it makes you feel needed. You then tend not to solve their problems, only support them in their problems. Real help breeds dependence on Jesus, not on you or me (Colossians 1: 28–29).

The vicious circle

Suffering from a poor self image can make you enter prematurely into marriage. Within marriage negative self image can cause all kinds of relationship and sexual frustrations, because it often goes hand in hand with an unacceptance of your body and physical attributes. A dreadful fear of failure (again due to false 'performance' evaluations of your worth) and the fear of rejection are often offshoots of a negative self image. Depression and a sense of loss, causing introversion, can all stem from this same root, and the more you look inwards and feel empty and lonely, and unable to receive or accept yourself, the worse it gets. Ultimately such depression can even lead, in extremity, to suicide. Hostility towards children can have its base in the same problem; if you don't/ can't love yourself, it's unlikely you'll find it easy to love the offspring of people like you.

None of this is helped by a society where unemployment is increasing, particularly amongst school leavers, bringing with it a sense of worthlessness, long hours of brooding, its denial of your chance to 'perform' and therefore by *society's* standards to 'prove' your worth. It ought to be true for the Christian that to be out of work need never mean to be unemployed— kingdom work always needs to be done. Allowing unemployment to foster a bad self image will hinder you and your prospects of employment because of the way that you present yourself at interviews or the way you have to chase interviews in the first place. Unemployment never helps self image. Being a Christian doesn't guarantee you a job. But it is possible to be both unemployed *and* have a healthy self image, and that's infinitely preferable to being unemployed and having a bad one, or even being employed and having a bad self-image.

Breaking the circle

If that's the true picture (and I believe it is), then it's a bleak one. It seems a hopeless vicious circle of, 'I don't/can't accept myself so I can't love God properly or see how he sees me, so I can't accept/love others properly, which means I don't receive back from them the love I need to accept myself....' But God *can* break into the circle from the outside. I've painted the negative side, let's now look at how we can come into all the fullness and love that God has for us; and through us for others.

First we have to really believe that it isn't sinful to love yourself. God's love, as described in 1 Corinthians 13, isn't boastful or proud or self seeking. It's possible to enjoy God's love and to love yourself, as well as to love others. There is a kind of self love that turns people inwards, a selfish narcissistic love. That's the kind of self love some people force themselves into despite real, deep-rooted self hatred. Such love hardens people behind selfish masks and their motto becomes: 'Look out for number one.' And some self love, far from being rooted in self hatred cleverly masked, really *is* proud and egotistical. But if we learn to accept *God's* love for us, and start to love ourselves with that kind of love, then we become selfless, not selfish. Able to stop looking inwards all the time. Able to receive. Able to give to others.

Selfless not selfish

Jesus is the supreme example of this kind of selfless self love. It's interesting that on a number of occasions in the gospels when Jesus serves and loves people, he does so immediately after making some of the most amazing claims about himself. But Jesus isn't conceited. His self acceptance and positive self image isn't selfish. It is based on the fact of the Father's love for the Son. It enables Jesus to be selfless. Look at this contrast of self acceptance and selfless giving in John 13:3–5, or in a statement about Jesus in Philippians 2:3–11. You can only love God and others properly when you've come to love yourself.

In fact, you and I are commanded throughout the Bible to love ourselves! Right through from Leviticus 19:18 to three of the four gospels (Matthew 22:39; Mark 12:31; Luke 10:27) comes the same command: 'Love your neighbour as yourself.' This *command* is in fact a double command. 'Love your neighbour. Love yourself.' Once you've understood and believed from scripture that it's not a sin to love yourself as God loves you, that it's liberating to you and to others, that 'worm theology' makes a mockery and nonsense of what Jesus died to accomplish in us, then we can begin to live out this often repeated command 'love your neighbour as yourself'. We love ourselves not in order to pamper ourselves in attitude or in lifestyle, but to enable us to love God and others better. Have a look at the references to this same command in Galatians 5:14; James 2:8; Romans 13:9; 1 Samuel 18:1. Ephesians 5:31–33 instructs husbands to love their wives as they love their own bodies. (Verses 28–29 of this chapter cover those physical and/or sexual problems that can arise from negative self image.)

How can we live out these scriptures? The key comes in Romans 15:7, where the command is to accept one another 'just as Christ accepted you in order to bring praise to God.' Humanly speaking Jesus himself was unacceptable. Everything was against him. There was nothing about his appearance that would make men follow him. He was born amidst rumours of illegitimacy. He was rejected and threatened from birth (Matthew 2). He was renounced by political and religious leaders. He associated with those who were unacceptable. His friends, who could have helped him most, abandoned him and betrayed him. Eventually even God himself, eternally coexistent with the Son, had to forsake Jesus, who had been willingly made sin for us. But Jesus was resurrected to glory, which means there's resurrection hope for you and me. Jesus was unacceptable to everyone. Except the Father. Jesus accepted the unacceptable; people like you and me. The ultimate solution to lack of self love is Jesus. Read 1 John 4:19.

The compassion of Jesus for you enables you to be compassionate towards yourself, to forgive yourself, and then be compassionate and forgiving towards others. The compassion talked of in Matthew 9:36 is the same root word used in Romans 12:8 about the gift of mercy. Now that's good news for breaking into the vicious circle created by poor self image. God's love and compassion can be *imparted* to you supernaturally, if you want it. All you have to do is ask, in faith, and receive (James 1:6; Luke 11:13). You need to learn to forgive yourself for past sins and failures if for no other reason than that Jesus has. Don't let Satan condemn you (Romans 8:1) because Jesus has paid *in full*. He's forgiven you; *forgive yourself*. (Hebrews 4:15–16; Hebrews 10:19–23.)

You may need to pray with someone over past hurts, fears and doubts about yourself. You may need release from rejection. You may need to repent of your sins of self hate, self pity, or bitterness, because they are sins. No one can alter the past, but God is the God of time and can invade, forgive and heal your past and your memories. In that way he can alter the effects of your past on your present. You may need to meditate on the scriptures I've quoted in this chapter. Maybe you just needed to hear that it's sin not to love yourself, and not the other way around! Or perhaps you need a few practical pointers to help you put this into practice for yourself with God's help.

Some practical tips

These practical tips work on two levels. The first level is personal. The second is interpersonal and relates to our place in the body of Jesus Christ, the church. Both are important answers to the problem.

First how can you overcome a bad self image once the Holy Spirit has given you a desire to love yourself, and you've received the necessary prayer and ministry from your 'Paul'—the person to whom you go for help, and with whom you can share anything? Since low self image often goes with a poor view of yourself physically, it can help if you start a physical hobby, such as squash, badminton, or swimming. Or try keep-fit, disco dancing, aerobics. When I was at school I was very fat, and suffered agonies of self hatred on the rugby field, the cross country track or at P.E. in the school gymnasium. As soon as I no longer had to do sports, I avoided them like the plague! And that's despite having lost two stones in weight and grown four inches. The immediate problem was removed, but the low self image remained. Once I discovered the truths I've been writing about in this chapter, I started (tentatively at first) playing badminton and squash and swimming. (I did these things badly at first, but I'd realized I had nothing to prove; if God accepted me, so should I, and others could do as they pleased!) I've discovered in life that the things you most fear seldom happen (although you can almost wish them into existence by being so scared, and the devil takes advantage of that) and that problems are best tackled head on, not side stepped or ignored.

What other steps can you take to combat this problem of low self image? Well, don't be alone. Put yourself in the way of happy things, people, events. Treat yourself to something you'll enjoy—a good film, for example. One word of caution—don't over compensate the depression by overeating or over-indulgence in anything that may become your master. Refuse those heavy thoughts that clog you. Substitute them with positive thoughts (Philippians 4:8). Use the Bible. When Nebuchadnezzar was beside himself in an agony of self doubt, rejection, sin and despair, he eventually turned to God in praise (Daniel 4:34). Praise is a very powerful antidote to depression and poor self image. Saul turned to music (1 Samuel 16:23), ministering to his emotions so that the realization of his relationship with an accepting God could come through and take precedence over his low self image and negative emotions. A spiritual high may be followed by depression and self abasement as happened to Elijah (1 Kings 19:4–5). But God knew that what he needed was simply rest, food and drink. And he provided them! God identifies with and ministers to the heart plea and the physical/emotional state of ordinary people like David in Psalm 31:9–13. As we co-operate with him, he *will* do something about such problems!

Be patient with yourself—these problems can take some time to work out, as we rebuild old bad thought patterns, habits and attitudes into new good ones. Seek the advice of close friends in Jesus. Remember that depression can deepen faith and character (1 Peter 1:7; James 1:3) not destroy it. Remember that there are always those in a worse state than you are. Pray for *them*. Get involved in *their* answer. Not in order to gain your worth, but in order to express the worth you *already* have.

Self worth and the church

Lastly, practical help with discovering your self worth comes when you find a place within the body of Jesus Christ on earth now, his church. It helps to feel accepted and loved when you're in the context of a group of people who accept and love you for who you are, and whom you can love and accept, and where you can find your special niche of service in both giving and receiving. That group of people should be your church.

God has a special role and place in his heart for young people as you can see throughout scripture, although it's true that adolescence is more a product of Western society than of Eastern. For example, in Jewish culture, at the age of thirteen at the ceremony of Barmitzvah, the young male becomes an adult and immediately eligible for marriage and inheritance. Nonetheless it's biblically true that God has a specific purpose for you as a young person. Young people are not the church of tomorrow; you are the church of today. Otherwise there won't be a church of tomorrow!

Within the church there are certain advantages and disadvantages in being a young adult. The disadvantages are a tendency to be looked down upon and not entrusted with responsibility; you may feel impatient, lacking in the perspective that time brings, wanting everything to happen yesterday; and sometimes you may be provoked by the attitude of those who are older and should be wiser. But the advantages are enormous, not least that God himself has a fondness for youth. Have a look at Jeremiah 1:1–10; Jeremiah 2:1–2; Psalm 110:1–3; Psalm 103:1–5; Joel 2:28–32; 1 Timothy 4:12; 1 Corinthians 16:10–11; 1 Peter 2:2; 1 Samuel 3:1–21; Deuteronomy 28:50; Proverbs 20:29; Ecclesiastes 11:9–10; 1 Kings 3:6–14; 1 Corinthians 14:20. That little lot should be enough to help your self image, because you as a young person have a place in God's scheme of things! It should be enough to show you that God often referred to restoring people who are old to the zeal, fervour and energy of their youth, either spiritually, emotionally or physically. Not only does he not bypass people who are young, but often he actually chooses them *because* they are young. King David was a teenager when God called him to be king. Jeremiah was less than twenty when he received God's call to be a prophet. Timothy, the disciple of Paul, was about seventeen. Mary, the mother of Jesus, was about sixteen at his birth. Jesus himself clearly knew what he was about by the age of twelve (Luke 2:49). And indeed he was only thirty-three when he was crucified. The zeal, enthusiasm, freshness, energy, trust and malleability (to the Holy Spirit) of youth is sorely needed in the church. In *your* church. Just as it needs to be tempered by the wisdom, experience, prayer and example of age. God's church is meant to be a family.

Bridging the generation gap

The problem is there are often family squabbles, or even divisions. Often these are over either the Holy Spirit and forms of worship or the generation gap. Both ploys are tactics Satan uses to cause division. You need to find your place in the body of Jesus Christ as a person, not just as a young person. There are clear teachings on how youth should relate to those who are older, and there are also teachings for those who are older in relating to youth. Look at Matthew 18:1–6; 1 Timothy 5:1; Matthew 19:13–14; Luke 2:24, 27; Mark 10:13–16; Titus 2:3–8; Luke 18:15–17; 1 Peter 5:5. It may be a good idea for the young people's fellowship to *not* all sit together in one group at the back lefthand side of the church! Try mixing (in pairs for moral support!) with the rest of the congregation. Suffer slow hymns and few choruses, and listen to stories of 'how it used to be'. Then you can tell stories of how it is now! You can lead youth services and teach choruses, serve by cleaning the church, collecting the books, or decorating old folks' flats and weeding their gardens.

Serving for the match!

You will find your place in the body of Christ (and your gifts in the Spirit) by trying things out and by serving. You will make mistakes along the way. But that's got nothing to do with age or youth; serving and making mistakes in service is a spiritual principle. It's how we grow. Be sure; you have a place in the body (1 Corinthians 14:26; Romans 12; 1 Peter 4:10). When you've tried everything you can in general service, then you will find your particular gifts in the Spirit and your place in the church. The positive qualities of youth need never leave you with God's help. The positive qualities of age *can* be grafted on to those of youth. But do remember, as we discussed earlier in this chapter, that your identity in Christ comes before your function in his body—you'll find your place in the body when you find your identity in Christ.

So there it is; seeing the need for positive self image. Receiving that truth into yourself through prayer and ministry. Then putting yourself in the way of building a healthy self love—both personally, and within the church. And why? So that you and I can be free to be the people God always intended us to be. So that we can love him and others more. God has only good for you and me. I need/want all I can get, for his sake, and so do you. Don't wallow in despair. Don't hurt in self pity, or rejection. Don't opt out of the body of Christ. Be healed, whole and healthy. That's what Jesus wants for you. A self image that reflects the image of Jesus and mirrors that image to others. And a functioning place for you in his body.

IO

Finger on the Button

War and the Power of Peace

Ask any group of young people what is the uppermost, predominant fear in their minds today, and you'll probably get the same answer as I do. War. A nuclear holocaust. Annihilation. The arms race.

I grew up (not all *that* long ago) in a society and age where nuclear war was a possibility but not a probability. It was an issue, but not an ever-present, oppressive fear. I've had to readjust my attitude to this issue because today it's become a real and immediate threat. The impact of this threat is *massive*—it's a very real issue to millions of ordinary people, and to none more so than young people.

Youth has inherited a mess from preceding generations. It seems to me that each generation thinks itself cleverer than the one previous, and wiser than the one following, yet you, the youth of today, have been handed a world where the prospect of total annihilation is greater than ever before. Also, of course, it is always the youth of any generation that has most to lose (unfulfilled hopes, dreams, ambitions—as yet unlived, unrealized lives) and having lost it, it's the destruction of youth that has the greatest effect on society by the absence of young people (as witness the setbacks in employment and the church, to name only two areas of society, after World War 1).

So I find tremendous fear, debate and pressure among young people on this subject. There's an almost fatalistic acceptance that within this current youth generation there will be a holocaust, accidental or deliberate. It's a bleak outlook. It's a dehumanizing, demoralizing and depressing forecast. It's a possible scenario for the future that currently holds probably millions of young people (there are 8.25 million people between eleven and twenty-five years old in the United Kingdom) under a bondage of fear, worry and anxiety, depression and a sense of futility and frustration.

There are two aspects that I'd like to examine. Is it a biblical scenario? And what is the Christian's response?

God's view on the world's end

First then, is it biblical? The Bible teaches very clearly that Jesus Christ is going to return to this earth. The teaching on a Second Coming is spread throughout Old and New Testament alike. It's found in Isaiah, Daniel, Joel and Malachi. It's there in the gospels, in 1 Corinthians and 2 Corinthians, in 2 Thessalonians and in Revelation. There are three New Testament words used to explain different facets of Jesus Christ's Second Coming. *Parousia* means the coming of a ruler, potentate or king, in authority and power. *Apokalypsis* means the unveiling or revelation of that which was previously hidden or obscured, now in all its power and splendour. And *Epiphaneia* means the visible reappearance of Jesus Christ. So the picture is of a King coming this time not as a child in a manger (the 'God-in-a-box' syndrome which the world trots out and commercializes from autumn onwards each year), but as Lord, revealed to all and appearing physically in a resurrection body to reclaim his creation.

The Bible is equally clear that while no one knows when this will be (so ignore anyone who says they do know), there will be certain identifiable signs (see Matthew 24), many of which are now with us. There will also be a time of 'tribulation', or enormous hassle, mainly under the direction of an economic, political and religious leader demanding total submission (including worship) across the world. This figure, endowed with supernatural (satanic) powers, is called variously the 'abomination that causes desolation' (Matthew 24:15), 'the man of lawlessness' (2 Thessalonians 2:3), 'anti-christ' (1 John 2:18, etc.) and the 'Beast' (Revelation 13).

It does seem clear to me that the church will be expected to go through this tribulation (Matthew 24:2, etc.). After this period Jesus Christ will return, reign and judge, and the resurrection of all the dead will take place. The Christian believes not only in spiritual union with Christ (Luke 23:43; 2 Corinthians 5:6), but also in a new resurrection body (1 Corinthians 15) to go along with the 'new heaven and a new earth' (Revelation 21). God is currently re-creating creation. Having started originally with the universe and the earth and finished with people (Genesis 1), this time in re-creation God has started with people (2 Corinthians 5:15) and will finish with a new heaven and earth. It's a mirror image. That's why Genesis with its garden, river and tree of the knowledge of good and evil is reflected at the opposite end of the Bible, in Revelation, with the River of Life, and the tree whose leaves are for the healing of the nations. And the central pivot point of this re-creation is, of course, Jesus himself.

So, whatever happens before this re-creation is complete, we know as Christians that God's grace and strength and courage are for us. And that we're on the winning side. I've read the last chapter, and the good news is: we win! It is also clear from Scripture that there will be an earth, and people, for Jesus to return to! So total annihilation is out—indeed God has never allowed total annihilation to happen, and nothing happens that he doesn't allow. (Much happens that he doesn't *want* to happen and it breaks his heart, but that's a different issue.) Even in the flood God preserved eight people, and promised not to do that again. The balance, though, is that in 2 Peter 3 there's a clear indication of some kind of massively scaled disaster, presumably the same kind of disaster that Jesus talks of in Matthew 24. That tribulation *could* end in nuclear war, but we don't know. We don't need to fear the outcome and we can do something about it here and now, instead of sitting and fretfully waiting, or merely piously opting out and praying without acting.

Fitting in with God's viewpoint

This second question: 'What is the Christian's response?' is a very difficult one. There's a verse in 2 Chronicles 9 which says, 'When the Queen of Sheba heard of Solomon's fame, she came to Jerusalem to test him with hard questions.' I feel rather like that in facing this issue, with the exception that I'm not Solomon, and don't have his wisdom. But then, I doubt that you are the Queen of Sheba either! So what I think we should do is confess our poverty in spirit (Matthew 5:3) and our lack of wisdom (James 1:5) and learn from God. Confidence in facing this issue can only come by revelation of Jesus Christ and through his book. We need clear thinking, a right heart and honesty.

Starting where we are at

I'd like to begin by examining briefly the situation that we inherited. Since 1945 we've had more than 130 wars, with some seventeen going on currently. We had our own taste of this during the Falklands crisis in 1982, and of course the shadow of Northern Ireland continues to loom large over the United Kingdom. You may remember or have learned of the near nuclear miss that took place at the Bay of Pigs, as America blockaded the Russian fleet's approach to Cuba, under the Presidency of John F. Kennedy. What isn't broadcast quite so much, probably because the information isn't safely 'neutralized' by the distancing of history, is the news that over an eighteen month period at the end of the 1970s, there were no fewer than 147 false nuclear alarms of major import. The time in this century when the world has actually been at peace constitutes only a few months. Every hour that passes, a further £42 million is spent on arms, (the same amount raised for Ethiopia by *Live Aid*) which means that two weeks' global spending on 'defence' could feed the world's hungry for a year. 22,000 major corporations exist for arms manufacture, maintenance and sales in the United States of America alone. War is big business.

Who wants war?

It has even been argued that warfare is desirable! It's a fact of history that many of the motives behind World War 1 were economic rather than political or territorial, and that economic considerations perpetuated if not initiated that war on *both* sides. George Orwell's frightening vision of the future, *1984*, has Oceania actually at war with either Eurasia or Eastasia, in order to maintain and preserve the economic and social balance of Big Brother's Party. Economic control has been and will remain a cause of war.

Another argument sometimes extended to justify warfare (on any scale) is its effect on the population. It has been estimated that the current economic and food situation worldwide would be far less stable than it is even now, had we not had two world wars. War is unarguably a great exerciser of population control.

Then there's the 'safety valve' of national and international aggression control. This is based on the theory that there's a kind of natural subconscious aggression muscle that, if un-flexed too long, results in sudden cataclysmic spasm, as evidenced by two world wars, the second occurring only twenty-one years after the world declared that such a catas-trophe must never be allowed to occur again. Some indication of the plausibility of this theory can, I think, be seen in the great nationalistic fervour incited by politicians and the media during the Falklands conflict, which was sufficiently far away and relatively unimportant to the welfare of the United Kingdom to enable the nation to flex its 'aggression muscle' without incurring too much personal danger. If this theory is correct, we are (on a global scale) well overdue for a cataclysmic spasm. It's argued that it may be better to have minor and continual conflict as a safety valve than to have peace leading to inevitable eventual world-wide 'spasm'.

Some political extremists advocate warfare on the grounds of nationalism and nationalistic expansionism, which I would define as patriotism gone mad! Nationalistic fervour seizes on people's jealousy, their pride, desire for dominance, or willingness to be subservient to their leaders. It whips up a kind of nervous tension, which is almost hysterical in its fervour. Its outlet can be seen in Hitler's Germany and the Nazi reaction to the Jews. Or in the IRA's reaction to the British Government. Or in the United Kingdom's reaction to Argentina in 1982. And so on. Should nationalistic expansionism be used to justify war, as it was in the days of the British Empire?

People have even tried to justify warfare in terms of its effects on unemployment. Or its creation of a kind of camaraderie that exists between people in the same fix. Many older people will tell you of the openness and friendliness of people united behind a common cause during World War 2. There is obviously some truth in this, albeit good brought out of bad, but I'd rather see people united behind Jesus than behind a war cause. I think also that the distancing of time adds a rather rosier glow to history than facts would indicate. The human mind has a tendency and ability to forget pain, fear and anxiety quite quickly, while highlighting and re-membering good aspects of the same incidents.

I do hope that in reading through the last few paragraphs, you've been knocking down these 'straw men' I've been setting up as arguments to justify the use of force and violence in warfare. They are arguments that are raised by politicians, economists, sociologists, and military strategists. Measured against the evil and the human cost of warfare and, as we'll see later, against God's own absolutes on violence, these are non-arguments. Even logically you'd have to be more concerned with pushing paper statistics than with people, to propagate such insanities in the first place.

Tricky issues not fatuous answers

There are, however, more tricky issues when it comes to the Christian's attitude to warfare, aggression, violence, and nuclear proliferation. These are not so easily dismissed—they relate to the possible justifiable *necessity* of war.

It must be said that there are people who hold fatuous, unthinking views on *either* side of the violence/pacifist debate. But it's futile to imagine that *all* those who believe in a justifiable war and permissible nuclear deterrents are simply nationalistic expansionists or warmongers. Just as it's equally futile to suggest that *all* those in favour of nuclear disarmament and passive resistance are simplistic and naïve. To adopt either of those attitudes is unhelpful, unChristlike, and simply reinforces prejudices and positions already adopted. Such attitudes do not enable you to form a decision. Once again our criteria for examining this question should be biblical ones. We must be honest and allow God to test our motives and reactions so that he can 'see if there is any offensive way in me' (Psalm 139:23–24).

A 'just war'

Many people have argued clearly and strongly in favour of a 'just war'. Early church fathers such as Ambrose, Aristotle the first, and Augustine defended such a position, and indeed the position of 'just war' became not only tenable but accepted from the fourth century onwards in church history. Significantly, in the centuries before that the church was decidedly anti-war. The idea of the 'just war' is defined as follows: that there may be a 'just cause' against a clear wrong (for example, Hitler and his Facist Third Reich in World War 2); that 'just means' could be employed to oppose the clear wrong (for example, the idea of proportionate violence inherent in the 'eye for an eye' attitude with biblical references such as Exodus 21:24; Proverbs 6:16–17; Deuteronomy 20:14; Isaiah 59:7–8; that 'just means' could proceed from a 'just intention' when the heart motivation and attitude are right (Deuteronomy 10). Pushed far enough along this line of thought 'just disobedience' is permissible covering both disobedience to government systems and also to God's general or personal precepts. The ethics of the Sermon on the Mount in Matthew 5 become general and personal only, not nationally or internationally applicable. A number of scriptural examples can be cited to support these views. John the Baptist's attitude to his society's overlords and his resistance to them, ending in his execution. Or the position of New Testament Christian soldiers in the Roman Praetorium Guard. Submission to authority set over us as in Romans 13:1–7 may have far-reaching implications during times of war.

A 'necessary' evil

Many Christians and non-Christians alike have gone beyond the concept of a 'just war' to the more general idea of the necessity for violence and warfare. Recognizing that we live in a real, fallen world, and that sin will always produce conflict, many people believe that the end (the overcoming of the conflict of sin) justifies the means (the use of violence). So many people believe the government needs violence to overcome violence (for example, baton charges against brick-throwing pickets, etc.). Christians should be salt and light in *all* of society, and that therefore includes the armed forces. Thus some Christians believe one can be actively involved with a clear conscience and can use force in the war against evil, oppression and wrong with the aim of spreading good, freedom and protection.

God's 'holy wars'

The third strand is the idea of a biblical, God-ordained holy war. The facts of such a position cannot be refuted, since they are recorded in Scripture often enough, and are sometimes cited as a model for our attitude to warfare today. But there are important differences between God's dealing with Israel in the Old Testament and his dealing with the new Israel and people in the New Testament. God hasn't changed, and there is no difference between the God of the Old Testament and the God of the New Testament. What has changed is our society and the strategic point we are now at in God's intervention in human history, post-Calvary.

In the Old Testament Israel had to be protected by God at cost, because they were a holy and chosen people, chosen to spread God's news, chosen eventually to produce Jesus Christ himself (Leviticus 11:44; Leviticus 20:23; Isaiah 6:13). Their warfare was clearly miraculous and directly ordained by God, not by technical or numerical superiority (Deuteronomy 20:1–9; Joshua 11:6–9) but by God's power. As God moved through human history in his progression towards a better new covenant relationship, so too the prophets (that is, God's chosen, spoken to and obedient people) increasingly protested against waged warfare (Isaiah 31:1; Nahum 2:13) and promised a coming era of peace (Zechariah 2:2–5; Zechariah 9:9–10; Micah 4:1–3). This refers to the new covenant relationship, a better way of fulfilling the law, to Jesus Christ himself, his teachings, including attitudes to warfare and violence, to the kingdom that's come and is coming. We are not left to work out each situation on its merits with few if any absolutes. God has given us Jesus Christ and the New Testament, and there are absolutes which I believe we should aim to live by in relation to this issue of war and pacifism.

God and situational ethics

Situational ethics are really a non-starter. Situational ethics confer responsibility for a situation or decision onto the shoulders of the participants and off the shoulders of God. They usually indicate unwillingness to trust God's ability to deal fairly and adequately with situations that are complex in their nature. When we find it difficult to trust, we tend to try to sort out the problem ourselves, rather than leave it in God's hands. Let me give a classic fictional example.

You stand at the bottom of a hill. A little girl runs past you in apparent distress. Shortly afterwards an obviously mad man holding a knife runs up to you, and asks which way the young girl went. Do you (a) lie? (b) tell the truth? (c) keep silent? (d) seek to restrain the madman?

The answer can, of course, be debated indefinitely, unless we refer to God's ideas on the matter, and then live by them. God says that we are not to lie. God hates liars (Proverbs 19:22; John 8:44; Revelation 21:8). So, even to produce a good result (mislead the madman and save the girl) we don't lie. We will want to restrain him, but we won't lie. If we do, if we tell a 'white lie', then in effect we're saying that God's absolute about telling the truth (Matthew 5:37) cannot always be right, good and workable. We are not trusting God to deal with the consequences of living according to his already revealed absolutes. So we take the responsibility back on ourselves and off God, and we do the opposite of what God has said we should do. And then the results become our responsibility, not God's. This is when it becomes dangerous and leads to eventual, if not immediate, foul-up.

Now transfer this situational ethic approach to war and peace. The issues are obvious. 'Should I fight in the event of war?' 'Are deterrence and defence O.K.?' 'Should I obey the Government in the event of a call to war?' 'Should Christians be in the armed forces?' We need to look for the absolutes. God is a God of practical, workable, absolutes. Most situational ethics occur when we don't like the absolute answer.

Answers, Absolutes, Alternatives

So what are the answers? What are the absolutes? Are there alternatives? Jesus ushered in a new age, and a new generation. Studies of the last days, or end times (called eschatology), point out that there is a time lapse between the bringing of God's kingdom through Jesus (his birth, life, death and resurrection drawing the kingdom to hand, putting it within your grasp) and the fulfilment of God's kingdom through Jesus (the Second Coming, resurrection of the dead and judgement). Nevertheless, we live now in a time of grace, when the kingdom of God with Jesus Christ as King, is being ushered in on earth as in heaven by the Holy Spirit. So Christian pacifists are not just non-activists or crassly naïve; the word pacifist is an active one—it means *peacemaker* (Matthew 5:9) and not just *peacekeeper*.

God's kingdom is radically different from earthly kingdoms, and indeed reverses many of the world's values (Luke 4:16–21). God's previous holy wars now give way, in an age of grace, to a time of delay, when evil is reserved for judgement (Romans 12:19–21). This kingdom has rules which apply to personal and political living (Luke 1:71–75). To reject Jesus, his lifestyle and his teaching inherently means rejecting the kingdom life, and choosing the way of war (Luke 19:41–44). God's plan for the world and its individuals is revealed in and through his Son Jesus Christ; it's a way of reconciliation and of resurrection to new life. Jesus is *the* example.

The cross of Jesus Christ is the ultimate demonstration of his plan, of course. It's a place of absolute equality. It's a place on which rests final, fair and merciful judgement. It's the place where love and justice meet. It's where in the face of oppression, threat, cruelty, even hatred, there is unilateral, undeserved forgiveness (Romans 5:8; Luke 23:34). It's Jesus' example to me. And to you. The cross is the living out of the teaching of Jesus—the cross, and the potential beyond it for resurrection and new life, is the answer to violence and warfare. The cross was the ultimate demonstration of Jesus' own teachings and lifestyle on these very issues. It takes the kick out of all the questions on situational ethics. It's not pleasant. It doesn't appear to work short term. But it *is* workable. It's the *only* solution long term. And it's God's way.

One way only

Of course, Jesus was tempted to bring in the kingdom in other ways (Luke 4:1–13). But there are no other ways to advance the kingdom of God other than Jesus' way (John

14:6). Jesus was destined to suffer (Mark 8:27–38), born to humility (Zechariah 9:9) and to suffering servanthood (Isaiah 53). His teachings are for us too. The command in Matthew 28:20 applies equally to us and means we, Jesus' disciples, should obey John 18:36; Matthew 26:51–52; Matthew 5:9; Matthew 5:38–48; Romans 12:14–21; 1 Peter 2:19–25. You can't get round these. Do look them up for yourself!

In my own life I need to apply these principles of undeserving forgiveness to others, whether they're individuals or nations. I need to consider if it can *ever* be in my enemy's best interests to kill him (is that loving your enemy?). It might be in his interests to oppose him, even physically to restrain or harm him (I'd rather break someone's arm than have them held responsible for killing me, or anyone else), but never to kill him. How can I deny him or her the opportunity for acceptance and conversion? I can never disobey God's instructions 'you shall not kill' (Exodus 20:13)—the actual Hebrew says 'kill' and not 'murder'.

So for me active involvement in the war machine (including participation in keeping it going indirectly) is out. For me this is in line with scriptural teaching in Matthew 22:17–22 and Romans 13 concerning God and human government. To be *subject* to authority does not necessarily mean to be *obedient* to that authority. Clearly allegiance to God comes first. If that contradicts human authority (and it often can, especially in places like Russia) then I resist the human authority, while remaining subject to it. If I'm against the law of the land on God's behalf, then I'm still subject to it; that means that I'll recognize its courts and I'll live with (some people have to die with) the consequences of disobeying that authority. Acts 5:29 and John 18:36 help elucidate this viewpoint scripturally.

What do I do?

The alternatives then are to examine ourselves and to be personally resurrected to kingdom values. To question what we're 'defending' with our defence taxes, our government policies, and why. All too often we're not defending good or God's kingdom, we're simply defending our lifestyle and possessions at the cost of our enemies' lives (or at the cost of the starvation of the Third World where money could be better spent).

An alternative is to pray. Ephesians 6:10–18 makes cl who the kingdom's enemies are and how to fight. I've ot explored enough how to wage warfare in spiritual realms through intercession. Have you? It is practical. It's not a cop-out. Go back to the chapter on prayer and praise (Chapter 3). Nor is it an excuse in the place of activity. Jesus resisted evil by bringing in good (see Mark 5). He resisted unfairness in Matthew 21:12–14; Matthew 23:13–39; John 18:19–24—his was the way of *active* non-violence.

I'm sure too that economic and social opposition through boycotts, embargoes, non-co-operation, peaceful picketing and demonstrations, petitions, political lobbying etc. haven't been fully explored by Christians who ought to be living examples for the rest of the world on these issues.

There are alternatives. Sometimes the issues look too big; how on earth do you tackle them? Well, how do you eat an elephant?! Answer—a bite at a time! How do we tackle the issue of bombs which, if it's immoral to use them, it's immoral to threaten to use them? How do we work out issues of peace and war? And law and order? Answer—a bit at a time, affecting society as Jesus affects us.

Hide, or go seek

Finally, to anyone reading this chapter and feeling that it's an area best avoided, let me implore you again to re-examine your attitude in relation to Jesus and his word. I know that wars and rumours of wars are inevitable (Matthew 24:6–7). I know that there'll be more war, not less, as time runs out for this present creation. But that's not a reason for steering clear. Because although I know that sin will never be eradicated this side of judgement, nevertheless it doesn't stop me aiming personally at Jesus' example (Romans 5:20–6:2). I know that some people will go to hell (Matthew 7:13–14), but it doesn't stop me working in evangelism to achieve God's desire (2 Peter 3:9).

So I'll encourage people to get involved in prayer and to adopt a personal lifestyle that reflects the way of the cross, the sacrifice of obedience and unilateral forgiveness. (After all, that's what this book is all about.) I'll encourage them to join the Christian Campaign for Nuclear Disarmament, and demonstrate peacefully and operate embargoes and the like. But don't let's forget that we only win long term when Jesus Christ comes back. All we do until then merely hastens his return, which is good, but the campaigning must not become an end in itself. Political activism must never and can never take the place of personal communion with Jesus Christ. Society changes when individuals change. Peace comes from God at the command of Jesus Christ in the power of his Spirit that is stronger than the forces of chaos and darkness (Mark 4:39). Peace isn't merely the negative cessation of war; it's the positive power of love and forgiveness. The power of the kingdom. It's the power of the cross.

11

It is Better to Give

God's Answer to Materialism

Every year we are horrified by television reports of famine, poverty and disease on a national scale. Ethiopia currently probably looms larger in our minds than most, perhaps because of the scale of the famine, the estimated millions who will starve to death, or the hard impact of vivid pictures and news reports.

Everyone is horrified by such reports. Some are stirred enough to actually do something about it (though all too often it's a one-off gift that relieves the conscience though not the famine). You don't need to be a Christian to be humanely moved by such disasters. But interestingly, it's mostly the non-Christians who blame God for such horrors. Working in schools during any such tragedy as the Ethiopian famine brings you in for a lot of stick if you're a Christian. 'Why does God allow it then?' 'If God's so good, why doesn't he do something about it?'

An involved God?

Poverty and the Third World is no longer easy to ignore. But God's desire for a solution means that Christians cannot ignore such problems. My God is not remote—he doesn't sit like some helpless grandfather with a long white beard and a

Marks and Spencer's white nightie, floating on a cloud way above all the pain and degradation of human suffering. God is involved in suffering. If you are distraught at scenes from Ethiopia, think how God feels. It's his world. He has total love for these people. He's so involved in the human condition that it cost him, in terms of suffering, the life of his Son, Jesus Christ. Suffering is a watershed; it always has the potential for either driving you towards your only ultimate source of help, or away from him.

A helpless God?

But if God is involved, is he helpless then? Why doesn't God alter it all? The question bears some examination, and we looked at it briefly in the chapter on witnessing. What can God do? If he removed all potential for suffering at noon today, which of us would be left at 12.01 p.m.? Answer—no one. Much suffering (including Ethiopia, despite the 'natural' disaster of drought) is directly man-made. The same issues of greed, jealousy, power lust, insecurity, fear and selfishness that rage in me and in you are the issues, on an international social scale, that through politics and governments determine the plight of more than one billion people currently stunted physically and/or mentally because of inadequate food. Man-made suffering means me. It means you.

So God will not at this stage just call a halt and wipe us all out. He loves us too much (including those who are suffering) and he wants everyone to have the maximum chance of repentance. He will call a halt eventually, but he's patient. Of course, he could impose his will upon us and make all of us do what he wants. The problem here is that the imposition of someone else's will upon our own doesn't actually produce good—it produces mindless, robotic blindness. There's no relationship in that. God is love, and love must always offer the opportunity of choice. Love demands relationship. God could make man change, but we'd then be something less than man, no longer true to the image of the Creator. And because of his love, he won't do that.

This idea of change in the individual is the key to God's solution to suffering. He created, through Jesus Christ, the potential for every individual to be changed, according to his desire, will and co-operation. Although God isn't willing for any to reject him and perish, many will. Consequently, this world order will remain corrupted until Jesus comes again, and so there'll always be both man-made suffering and 'natural' suffering (earthquakes, drought, disease, etc.) until such time. But God's love and involvement means there is the potential for change here and now, as you and I bring in God's kingdom here on earth.

Bringing in the kingdom

Let me start big and then narrow down to the personal. I know of multinational corporations that have had policy changes effected by the prayers and peaceful boycotting of oppressively financed products by whole communities of Christians. Faced with powerful business magnates we can often feel insignificant and helpless, but remember that God is in the business of redeeming principalities and powers (earthly ones as well as heavenly) and making them all subject to Jesus Christ (Colossians 1:16–20). So we needn't fear the giant companies. Our attitude should be one of reclamation; we should reclaim these runaway godless ventures for Jesus! And we do that by involvement. As God's people you and I are called out of the sin of the world, not away from the sinners. We are not of the world but we are in the world (John 17:13–21). Letters and phone calls, protests and boycotts, prayer and fasting, parliamentary lobbying and personally adjusted lifestyles with selfless giving can all be used against injustice and oppression. Do you know who your M.P. is? When did you last write to him concerning the government's attitude to immigration, or third world famine relief, or defence spending? In our present democracy it is still amazing how M.P.s will jump if constituents (particularly a good number of them—your church, for example) write and protest. Get the name and address of your M.P. at the local library. You need to keep informed—buy a daily paper, listen to or watch the news, vote in elections if you're allowed to.

Let me narrow the scope a little. Apart from a spiritually practical onslaught on the world's order of affairs, there are lots of opportunities for you and me to be involved even more personally through Christian agencies such as TEAR Fund. Such agencies provide opportunities to sponsor a child's living standards and education and schemes to support missionaries who give their lives in practical and spiritual service.

Jubilee for now!

Of course, supporting these kinds of issues, both the wider ones of lobbying international governments over issues of justice and freedom and the more personal involvement in relief agencies, will have an immediate impact on your time, energy, and your wallet! There is personal cost involved. That's good and as it should be.

In the Old Testament God operated a principle called Jubilee. Every few years various debts would be cancelled and goods owed, or slaves in service, would be 'redeemed'. But every fifty years, or Jubilee, all debts were cancelled and all oppression lifted. In the New Testament Jesus declared he was bringing in a new and perpetual state of Jubilee. That's what's behind Jesus' reference in Luke 4:18–19 to Isaiah 61:1. Jubilee is the acceptable year of the Lord. You and I are living to demonstrate the same release of captives, the same freeing from cruel injustice and oppression. Jubilee is for now.

I'd like to concentrate on just one area of cost, and that's financial cost. (Please don't skip these next few paragraphs. They're important.)

We live in a third of the world that has two-thirds of the world's resources. Our society with all its problems and deprivations is affluent. Income, salary and personal budgeting remain one of the few 'taboo' subjects in British society. You can talk about politics, sex, even death and religion, but don't mention finance! Now, I won't mention your income, whether it's from pocket money, a part-time job, a full-time job, or from the Department of Stealth and Total Obscurity, except to say that *you and I are rich*. And please don't do what I've done before; immediately look around for someone getting more than I am, so that I can say, 'I'm not rich, look at him.' If you want to draw comparisons, look at the Indians in Pakistan going blind because they can't afford £1.50 for simple eye treatment. Look at the one in six child mortality rates in Liberia, because parents can't afford food. Look at Ethiopia. Look at two-thirds of the world's population, 'living' below both poverty and starvation levels.

It's better to give...

What can we do with our relative riches then? In the Old Testament God laid down certain very clear rules and guidelines concerning giving. The laws of Jubilee (Leviticus 5:10–27:34) were one set. Looking after aliens and foreigners (Leviticus 19:34; Deuteronomy 10:19), the poor, orphans and widows (Exodus 22:22; Deuteronomy 24:17; Proverbs 23:10–11; Jeremiah 7:6) were also included. Looking after God's chosen ministers and priests (Leviticus 6 and 7) was another principle laid down by God. *None* of these laws were revoked in the New Testament in principle; Jesus came to fulfil the law and improve it under a new covenant of grace, not to abandon the law (Matthew 5:17–20). Where previously the law dealt with externals, the grace of God now brings freedom and deals with our heart's attitudes internally. We have less excuse to fulfil God's care-standards for others (Christian and non-Christian) not more.

How about you?

In the Old Testament the personal minimum was a tithe (ten per cent) from first fruits (that is, before any kind of taxation) plus gifts and offerings (see Leviticus 27:30–34; Deuteronomy 12:17; Deuteronomy 14:22; Malachi 3:10–12). So it must be a personal minimum for now too. Of course in the New Covenant everything we have is God's (including possessions, money, time, etc.), so a tithe plus gifts as outlined above should therefore become our minimum. Jesus clearly expected us to be involved in giving, hence his throwaway comment in Matthew 6:2, '*When* you give to the needy,' and not, '*If* you give.'

So let's nail it right down. Are you tithing? I've heard all kinds of arguments from Christians about how this is an Old Testament principle, not a New Testament one. And the interesting thing is, I've always discovered that people arguing that way are actually arguing to give less than their tithe. Never more. Forgive me, but I sometimes wonder about commitment and motivation here. God's people often only give (time, finance or whatever) when they see blessing, and not before. Am I like that? Are you? Isn't it still true that if I'm committed to something, then that's where you'll find my money going? Jesus said that I can't serve two masters; Mammon (the god of material wealth) and God—I'll hate the one and love the other, or be devoted to the one and despise the other (Matthew 6:24). I should be hating the hold that money can have on my faith, my commitment, my lifestyle, my selfishness. Jesus said that where my treasure is, that's where my heart will be (Matthew 6:19–21). Is my treasure in heaven or the Co-operative Bank? The reverse is equally true; where my heart is, is where I'll invest my 'treasure'. Is it in righteousness and justice, or in selfishness and oppression? Jesus said these things to you too.

I'll never forget the deep impression a visiting speaker made on me at a University Christian Union meeting. I'd not long been a committed Christian, and the Rev. Philip Hacking came to speak on tithing. The one phrase which stuck with me was this: 'Would people be able to tell from an examination of my cheque book stubs that I was a Christian?' It's not perhaps a primary test of how your Christianity works, but it is a valid one.

I know most of the excuses against tithing: the 'scriptural' excuse, 'It's only for the Old Testament' and the 'practical' excuse, 'I can't afford to tithe'. I know them because I've tried them! But you can't afford *not* to tithe. It's nonsense to say you haven't got ten per cent of your income; you have it by definition. It's what you do with it. And if you're living to the limit of your financial income without tithing, then you're living beyond God's limit for your income, because you're meant to tithe. It doesn't matter how much the tithe is in money: it's the principle of giving sacrificially that's important. Your 50p per week is every bit as important as someone else's £15 (Mark 12:38–44).

God's 'accounting' for suffering and poverty

There are incredible amounts of money available for God's budgeting to extend his kingdom, but much of it is either lying safely idle in Trust Accounts or in Building Society Funds 'just in case', saved 'for a rainy day'. It may even be lying in my pocket, bank account or building society. Or in yours. It's not wrong to save, but it is wrong to 'hoard' money at the expense of others' poverty. It is wrong to budget without God. It is wrong to live luxury-filled lives whilst others starve. It is wrong to 'spiritualize' Jesus' teaching on money and his attitude towards the poor and the rich (Matthew 13:22; Matthew 19:16–26; Luke 6:24–25) and to pretend that Jesus was only talking about our 'willingness' to give money, instead of actually giving it! Money isn't evil in itself, but love of money is a root of all kinds of evil (1 Timothy 6:10). Unless God specifically calls you to deal with lots of money responsibly, money will almost certainly tempt you, and very likely become your god.

Theoretically it should take only ten wage earners' average incomes to support one person in full-time Christian work. Or for those same ten people to support about ten more people in the Third World to bare living standards. *Why* aren't we doing more?

Prayer in action

Every time you or I pray the way Jesus taught us to in Matthew 5:9–13 we are asking for these very kinds of issues to be resolved through us. Look at the model Jesus left us....

The Lord's Prayer starts with the focus of life in the right direction—God first, us second. God as an intimate Father, the Abba/Daddy of little Jewish children greeting their fishermen-dads on the quayside after a hard day's work. It goes on to give God not only the intimacy of this love relationship, but also the reverence due to his holy name which shows that you and I are proud to be his children and to own him as Father.

Note the first request in the prayer is that God's kingdom (where there is no poverty, no suffering, no injustice) and his will should come about here on earth. This kingdom of heaven stuff isn't just 'pie-in-the-sky-when-you-die'. It's 'steak-on-the-plate-while-you-wait!'

The next request is intensely personal. I used to feel guilty about praying this part of the prayer every Sunday morning, one hour before tucking into Sunday roast at home. I didn't seem to need to ask God to give me daily bread! I had bread and more besides, each day. Have you ever felt like that? Well, you needn't! The whole of the Lord's Prayer is in the plural: 'Give *us* today *our* daily bread.' For as long as there are Christian brothers and sisters (in the family of the church) and non-Christian brothers and sisters (in the family of mankind, and created in God's image) who don't have daily bread, then you and I can pray this prayer with passionate reality. It's not just for me. It's not just for you. Nowadays I only feel guilty praying this when I'm not doing something about the answer, because you and I are part of God's answer to the problems of suffering, famine and disaster.

The rest of the prayer goes on to ask for forgiveness so that the enemy cannot accuse us and find our hearts condemned by wrong actions or our lack of right actions. Even here, although sin and forgiveness is intensely personal, the prayer remains plural, stressing my need to forgive others (who don't 'deserve' it) if I want to be forgiven. Prayer for guidance and deliverance, together with a positive profession of God's glory and power, round the prayer off.

That's the way to pray! It's also a stimulus to action given that any prayer will get you involved in its answer. (See the chapter on prayer and praise.) That kind of prayer will help regulate your attitude to the Third World, poverty, riches, disaster, and giving. And to our personal intervention, as well as God's.

Your money *and* your life

That leads me to the closing section that I'd like to look at briefly in this chapter. I guess I'm narrowing the scope of the chapter down still further from world issues through personal possessions to persons. To you and me. You see, God not only wants our time, our money, and our possessions, he wants us. He wants us to be personally involved, not just in giving and then thinking we've done our bit. That's rather like knocking on doors for one week in our church's Mission, and thinking we've done our witnessing, instead of being a witness twenty-four hours a day, seven days a week, fifty-two weeks a year. For life.

God wants you and me to be involved so much that he has already personally commissioned you. We've looked at it before in this book. Matthew 28:16–20 is your Great Commission. You say, 'That's for the Apostles.' The Bible says that it's for Jesus' disciples; you and me. You don't need to wait to be told to get involved; you've been commissioned already. In fact, unless you go (which is the command) you and I had better have a good reason for staying put. When I received a 'call' into full-time Christian service it was partly through knowing in my heart that nothing else would do. Because God had said to me 'go!'. For me it wasn't to be abroad, but from rural Lancashire to inner city London. For you it may be different again. But God does want you to be part of his solution to suffering.

There are enough Christian organizations to help you fulfil

his command from denominational and non-denominational missionary societies (like the Baptist Missionary Society or Horizons) through to relief agencies (like TEAR Fund) and youth orientated groups (like Youth with a Mission, Operation Mobilization and British Youth for Christ). A week of your life? A month, or six months? A year? Or your whole life-span? The principle is giving and going. The benefits are 'out of this world' because when you give, you receive (Acts 20:35). When God says where and when, go. It's the safest most privileged and 'frighteningly' secure place to be! You do the possible, and let God do the impossible. You can't exercise faith doing what you can cope with. You can only exercise faith doing what God has told you to do and which you can't cope with.

In this chapter I've tried to move through three phases of involvement in the issues we've looked at here. I believe all three are necessary and vital. Please don't feel guilty if you, like me, often fail in one or more of them. But please do, under God, *do* something about them.

12

Keeping on Track

Faith Is for You

Ever since the age of about six, I've been interested in puzzles, conundrums, word play, conjuring tricks and lateral thinking. Perhaps it's because I'm a lateral thinker, or I just have a devious mind, but I like to approach a problem from abstruse angles and find a quick or easy solution! Later, that same approach led to my being interested in conjuring, illusions and escapology, a hobby which I'm still actively involved in.

Few short cuts

I soon discovered, however, that in the Christian life there are no short cuts to growth and maturity in Jesus. Beyond keeping Jesus central, keeping things simple, learning lessons bit by bit and being kept in God's generosity there are very few short cuts. But if there are any, I certainly want to discover them. To be more like Jesus quicker and yet just as thoroughly has got to be a good target! I have, however, discovered over recent years that there are certain keys to unlock doorways to maturity in Christ, or if you prefer, there are power points that you and I need to plug into. They're not short cuts, but they should be vital ingredients in your life if you want that life 'to the full' (John 10:10).

Power points in God

What are these power points? Prayer and fasting, worship and praise, and the gifts and the fruit of the Holy Spirit are among them. But the subject of this chapter—*faith*—is absolutely fundamental to our pursuit of godliness.

For many years faith was a very intangible substance in my thinking. I knew it was very important, but I wasn't sure what it was, what it was for and how it worked. I've recently come to realize that faith is in fact a very practical, measurable commodity. It's practical because faith gets things done in power and authority (people get healed, prayers get answered, money gets given, etc.) and its' measurable because the more we grow in faith the more God can do through us. Remember in the chapter on prayer I talked about God needing to change us sometimes in order to answer our prayers? Well, one of the main changes God aims at is the building of faith in us. Faith is the channel through which God pours his Holy Spirit, or if you're still thinking about power points, faith is the fuse through which God directs his power. Faith isn't the power itself, nor is it the only fuse, but faith is certainly one of the carriers of God's power. Increase that fuse capacity and God can use you to carry more power for his kingdom. That in itself is a pretty nifty reason for seeking God for more faith. But let's take a step or two back and look at the whole issue.

Defining your terms

I suppose the most well-known definition of faith is found in that great biblical book about faith: Hebrews. The clearest definition comes in chapter 11 verse 1, where faith is described as 'being sure of what we hope for and certain of what we do not see'. That's not wishful thinking where you 'hope it'll all pan out O.K. in the end'. It's not even just believing in your *mind* that 'God is still in charge'. It's talking about real trust. The key words in that verse are 'sure' and 'certain', being absolutely sold out mind and heart that God *is* faithful and just. There's the crux of the matter; faith isn't something you acquire across heaven's counter ('Can I have half a pound more of faith please?'). Ultimately, it's not how much faith you have, but what you do with the faith you have got. Look at the parable of the talents (Matthew 25:14–30); invest wisely what you have and put it to use, and God will give you more. Jesus made it clear that faith the size of a mustard seed (deliberately one of the smallest seeds) can move mountains provided it's invested in the One who is faithful (Matthew 17:20). It's not your faith that matters, but who you have faith in. It's not that you have the faith, but that God is faithful. Let's get the focus right. For example, you never met a Christian full-time worker who lived 'by faith', but you may have met many who live 'by the faithfulness of God'.

That's why faith is based on being sure and certain. It doesn't have to do with our frame of mind or feelings, but is an integral part of the character, nature, and personality of our God; *he is faithful* (1 John 1:9). All we have to do is learn to plug in to that faithfulness in order to have our capacity for faith increased.

Unbelief: faith's opposite

Faith operates on different levels in our Christian lives, but the Bible is clear that it is a very vital ingredient. You can't get much clearer than: 'Everything that does not come from faith is sin' (Romans 14:23), or: 'Without faith it is impossible to please God, because anyone who comes to him must believe that he exists and that he rewards those who earnestly seek him' (Hebrews 11:6). So every time you or I affirm the problem of our circumstances instead of the provision of Jesus Christ, we are in sin. There are no negatives in the kingdom of God. Unbelief, cynicism and lack of faith are all sin; they hinder the building of the kingdom. It doesn't please God. We need to deliberately and consciously place our faith in the One who is faithful and keep focused on him.

Think of your Christian life like a railway journey; the engine that powers the whole thing, that keeps you going in the right direction at the right speed, is *faith*. The fuel for your faith in the tender immediately behind the engine is *fact*. And lastly chugging along in the rear is the carriage of your *feelings*. I'm not suggesting in good evangelical tradition that you learn to ignore your feelings. If you do that you are ignoring a part of your life that God created in his image—he has feelings too. I am asking you to let faith, not fact or feelings, do the driving. God wants to redeem your intellect (Romans 12:2) and your feelings (Ezekiel 36:26–27), not abandon them. When fact and feelings are in line, that's great, but when your circumstances or feelings put the brakes on your spiritual railway journey with God, then remember that it's faith that keeps you going forward. Without it you can't please God. And remember too, we can have faith because of the faithful nature of God.

I sometimes do a little experiment in classrooms to explain what faith in God is about. There's always someone foolish enough to volunteer and thus provide me with a co-operative victim!

Faith in action

I'll get this guy to face the classroom wall, hands by his side, feet together, face forward. Then I'll instruct him at the count of three to fall over backwards, keeping absolutely straight and stiff. Of course, I assure him that I'll catch him! Then I make it obvious by my voice that I've moved to the other side of the classroom and am counting from there! Not surprisingly this causes the volunteer some little consternation. What usually happens is that on the count of three (by which time I'll be sure to be quietly back behind the guy ready to catch him) the volunteer falls over halfway and then puts out his foot to stop himself going over. Lesson? He doesn't trust himself to fall back in my arms. If I'm not trustworthy then there's risk involved—it takes some bottle to do, although the more the guy knows me the easier it gets, because he *knows* that I won't let him fall and crack his head open. (Honest!)

Faith is having sufficient knowledge in your heart (not just your head) that God will catch you because he's faithful. Faith is 'belief mixed with trust wrapped up in action' because faith which does not demonstrably work has no value, and very quickly ceases to be faith at all. The more weight you put on the faithfulness of God the better it is.

Can you stand one more example? I average approximately two to three escapes a year from a strait-jacket while suspended upside down at a height of 100 feet from a crane. (If you want to know why, it's because it's my hobby and I use it to talk about the freedom from sin that only Jesus Christ can bring.) Now the thing that stands between me and a 100-foot drop onto my head is a specially-made foot harness. It's made from seat belt webbing that won't rip or tear. It's furnished at both ends with a fixed loop created by doubling the webbing back on itself and glueing, sewing *and* riveting it in place. During the escape attempt these fixed loops become running loops by threading the rest of the webbing through the fixed loop at both ends. These two 'lassoos' then go one over each foot and the middle of the harness is shackled to the crane. As soon as there is any weight placed on the harness, the running loops tighten round my ankles. The more weight, the tighter the harness on my legs, so the safer I am. Now you may be sure I checked the *facts* of that harness out when I had it made. Intellectual suicide was not for me! I checked the sewing, the glue, the rivets. You may be equally sure that my *feelings* were inclined to keep me on firm ground, not dangling that height from a crane! But at the end of the day the harness only worked when I *trusted* my weight to it. There had to come that point when I let go and the harness took over, and the strange thing is that the more I trusted the harness, the safer it got and the better its hold on me.

The point is obvious. Check the facts, don't be hampered by negative feelings. Put your trust in God—the more weight you put on him the safer things are. God is faithful.

Saving faith

Every single one of us has the capacity for faith. For a start Ephesians 2:8 makes it clear that we are saved by grace *through faith*, and since God is unwilling that any should perish, and since Jesus died for all, then we *all* have the potential for faith in God, although we don't all exercise that potential. This is one level on which faith operates: *saving* faith sufficient to trust that Jesus Christ died for my sins and is alive now to restore me, forgiven, to my Father God.

The gift of faith

Then there's the specific gift of faith, a grace gift from God through his Holy Spirit clearly listed in 1 Corinthians 12:9. That's the special kind of faith that in tough circumstances gets the impossible done. It's a gift; you can only ask for it, receive it and then exercise it. You don't exercise that type of faith until you've received it gratefully. It's the faith that George Müller exercised, or Dr Barnardo, or more recently the groups of Christians in the south of England who prayed in, through the gift of faith, £600,000 in a matter of months to start a drug rehabilitation centre and outreach ministry that God had laid on their hearts. What God burdens you with he'll equip you for, often making you the answer to your own prayers.

Everyday faith

But somewhere between these two levels of faith (saving faith and the specific gift of faith) is what I call relational or communion faith, that faith which is the basis for your ongoing friendship with Jesus. It's that level of faith that God is constantly looking to increase in you, more than you are looking to have it increased. God is committed to be the author and the perfecter of our faith (Hebrews 12:2). Are there ways, then, that we can plug into this power point to co-operate with his building in our lives? How can we increase our faith in the faithfulness of God?

Building your faith

Well, the first thing to realize for yourself is that all these power points are wired in together. You cannot increase faith in a dynamic and effective way without spending more time in prayer and fasting. Not in a legalistic way, but because this builds your relationship with Jesus. Similarly, if you grow increasingly free in praise and worship, learning gradually to trust your emotions to a God who's very emotional about you, so too your faith level will go up. Experimenting reverently but in a lively way in the gifts of the Holy Spirit and seeing him produce fruit in your life, and from it building your faith. They're all linked. Remember *Star Trek?* I'm reminded of Dr McCoy's sick bay on the USS Enterprise. The general health of the patient there was measured by a row of indicators that visually recorded the level of heartbeat, respiration, nervous system, etc. Sometimes it would be handy (and embarrassing!) to have the levels of our prayer and fasting, praise and worship, gifts and fruit, and faith life revealed. They are all linked and you can't build faith in isolation. Hence the reason for these particular chapters being included in this book!

There are just three pointers I'd like to offer you which are very simple and practical. If you want them to, I guarantee that these will build faith within you.

By hearing

First, God can build faith in you by *'hearing'*. The fancy name for it is impartation. God can and will impart to you faith. He will school you gently but firmly in the things that affect his very own heart. I for one need more and more of that kind of impartation. Jesus was constantly battling to wean his disciples off fear and onto faith. Reread Mark's gospel with that in mind and you'll see how the whole of that book is partly about the struggle to do just that. Faith and fear, like oil and water, don't mix. In Mark 4 we have the episode of the boat in the storm, marked by the disciples' fear. In Mark 5 we have the faith of the woman healed from a haemorrhage and Jairus' daughter surrounded by fear and unbelief. In Mark 6 we see Jesus hampered in the work of his Father's kingdom at Nazareth because of unbelief, and so on it goes. Unbelief is the opposite of faith. That was Gideon's problem in Judges 6 and 7. To cope with past failures in prayer and personal sins we build up a rationale to explain away such failure. We begin to develop a theology based on lack of power and experience. We develop the 'faith' that it won't work. That's sin. It's negative and not the values of the kingdom. We need to repent of it and look to build the positives of *real* faith that leads to success for the kingdom.

If you look in the gospels at what affected the heartbeat of Jesus you get a clear clue as to his character and what God values as being important. The cities, the poor, the diseased, the outwardly religious, faith—these are some of the things that burdened Jesus' heart while here on earth. I vividly remember, at a time when Jesus was doing much clearing out in my life, cycling into college one day and suddenly realizing that, as the temple of the Holy Spirit, my eyes could see things with the eyes of the Holy Spirit, the eyes of Jesus Christ himself. *I* could see/think/feel/do what Jesus would see/think/feel/do because I belong to him and his Holy Spirit lives in me. We *need* more of Jesus' perspective on situations if we are to move on in faith, and God will *impart* that heartbeat to us. We need to 'hear' in order to build faith, simply because Romans 10:17 says 'faith comes from hearing the message, and the message is heard through the word of Christ'. But how does this work?

Getting the head-heart drop

Suppose, for example, you have a hassle with faith over trusting that you're forgiven. O.K. You know in your head that 'faith comes from hearing the message and the message is heard through the word of Christ'. How do you get that vital eighteen-inch head-to-heart drop? Well, you know the written word of Christ is found in the Bible. So go through the Bible with a concordance (see the chapter on Bible reading) and highlight or underline every reference to forgiveness, marking it at the side with a little 'f' for forgiveness so that you can pick the references out quickly later. The same would apply to any faith hassle you had with healing, or with God as your Dad. Find the appropriate passages and mark them. Then, just as you would take medicine, read them three times a day. Memorize the easier ones for meditation, but (and this is important) ask the Holy Spirit to quicken these verses to your spirit in order to build faith, claiming the black-and-white promise of Romans 10:17. Remember that God's word is food and always achieves its purpose (Isaiah 55:10–11) and that it is a sword capable of getting right to the heart of the matter (Hebrews 4:12). I can't say more than that this *does* work; I've tried it. Faith does come in this way if you read appropriately asking *specifically* for faith from the verses via the Holy Spirit.

By seeing

Secondly, faith comes not only from hearing but from *seeing* or by revelation. Look at Paul's prayer for the Christians at Ephesus (Ephesians 1:17). When you've heard something from the word of God and it's been fed into your spirit by his Holy Spirit, you can grow faith from that. Similarly, when you've had a *personal revelation* or seen an aspect of God's character and how he wants to work in a given situation, then you can build faith on that too. Because God is constant and faithful, the personal revelation of his nature and faithfulness will inspire faith in you. 1 John 1:9 becomes real for you when you see how loving, merciful and just God is.

Let me be more specific and practical. When I was one year into my ministry with Youth for Christ I went through a period of intense depression. It was brought on largely through my own stupidity, partly through circumstances around me. I'd been living alone in a flat, not eating properly, away from the north of England where my home and friends were, working on my days off, doing an average of ninety hours a week, and a lot of it in my own strength and not God's. My girlfriend had just called a halt to our relationship, and my car had just been written off. In addition my friend and colleague was also going through a rough patch. Things were not easy! I was exhausted physically, spiritually and emotionally. After a period of time off work I was eventually able to go back to church, sitting at the back and leaving early because I couldn't cope with people's questions, or their genuine concern. Then, one day, and I can't say what the turning point was, as I sat in church depressed and feeling a million miles from God, unable to pray or worship, he gave me a personal revelation of his great love for *me*. He called me 'Peter', when everyone else called me 'Pete', and the picture he gave me in my mind was one I also felt in my heart. I saw myself before his throne, and while I didn't see God himself, I did see Jesus standing shoulder by shoulder with me. Jesus' arm was round my shoulder, and I'll never forget the firm, rock like strength of that grasp, yet the gentleness of its love. God was showing me that when he looked at me he saw Jesus, and when he looked at Jesus, he saw me. We were so close, Jesus and I, that we could no longer be separated or viewed as separate.

Now in print that may not sound anything special to you, but the reality of it still moves me, because it was a *personal* revelation. It built my faith that God still cared, still loved me, still understood. And it hasn't been an isolated incident restricted to moments of desperation. You can feel God and have personal revelation to build faith; when you see from God's perspective and know how he wants you to act/think/feel, then you can launch out in total faith. You *can* trust what he shows you.

Seeing is believing

Another example that built my faith through revelation happened at Spring Harvest 1984. I'd been counselling a couple for half an hour and got nowhere with finding the root of the girl's problem. We were starting to go around in verbal circles, and I shot up a prayer to God: 'Lord, I haven't got a clue; tell me what the problem is.' Almost immediately I felt the Lord say, 'Ask her what happened when she was five.' Now I did what you would have done; being a man full of faith, I bottled out! It took another five minutes of my asking the Lord to show me the problem, and him saying the same thing before I finally plucked up the courage to ask the girl what happened when she was five! (And if you don't 'hear' from God like that, look back to the chapter on prayer and the one on the Holy Spirit and commitment, because we're talking here about specific gifts of knowledge, walking by the Spirit, and learning to have a close walk with Jesus.) Anyway, as soon as I asked her, she burst into tears! I thought I'd really blown it. Here's Pete, the careful counsellor, and having asked her a question she bursts into tears! But it transpired that through a traumatic hospitalization at that time that there were some blocks that needed shifting in her life.

Lesson for me? God had *shown* me personally what the problem was through a word of knowledge, and if God *shows* me I can trust him and have faith for the results. If I pray for healing for someone, my faith must rest on what I see God wants to do in an individual's life. I don't pray for healing on the basis of a person's need, but on the basis of what I see Jesus wants to do there and then. So when a guy wants Jesus to heal him from asthma and sinus problems at Royal Week 1983, I see a picture in my 'heart's eye' of Jesus reaching out to touch the lad's chest (not his nasal passages). His chest is what I have faith to pray for, and that's what Jesus healed. The nasal passages were subsequently healed, because the *lad's* faith grew enough for *him* to ask Jesus to heal his sinuses. Jesus healed to the extent that the lad no longer needed his asthma spray, and the next day was running a seven mile marathon! Ask Jesus to *show* you by revelation what you can trust him for, what he wants to do in any given situation, and then when he shows you, boy can you have faith for that!

By doing

Third and finally, you build faith not just by hearing and seeing, but also by *doing* or demonstration. It's no good whatever sitting on your backside asking God to build faith in you and not doing anything about it. James 2:20, 26 puts it exceptionally clearly: 'faith without deeds is useless [dead].' Faith has to have a practical application in order for it to be faith at all. God won't pour into you if you aren't prepared to learn how to pour his goodness out onto others, Christian and non-Christian alike.

When we're talking about building faith, this means that you have to put yourself into the way of receiving faith. You have to go out on a limb for God. If you constantly stay in a place where you can cope, because you've done it all before and it worked out O.K., how are you ever going to prove that God is faithful? If you really want to build faith, this is where (as an Americanized friend of mine says) 'the rubber hits the road!' Hearing and seeing you can do in the comfort and security of your own home or fellowship group. *But* faith without deeds is dead, and you and I need to get out there and exercise it. Go out on a limb for God in a situation that you know is risky, not to test God but to demonstrate to yourself first and others second, that 'he exists, and that he rewards those who earnestly seek him' (Hebrews 11:6).

Faith for...

For each one of us building faith through action will take different forms. For some it will be a faith to pray out loud, for some a faith to be a youth leader or to love your parents, for others the faith to witness for Jesus Christ. But whatever it is, put yourself in the way of having to do something that will stretch you. Try something that's a bit beyond where you're currently at spiritually/emotionally/physically/mentally. God longs to stretch us, to build us, to key us into his power. Be practical. Set yourself faith targets in the different areas of your life that you know could do with growth and maturity.

If you aim at nothing, that's exactly what you'll achieve. But when you attain a faith target with God's help, you will have more faith for the next target which is further ahead.

The storm of doubt; the trial of faith

Remember 1 Peter 1:7 tells us that God delights in the refining of our faith; it's of greater worth to him than gold. Your faith *will* be tested—not smashed or tempted, but tested. When that happens, don't do what I all too often do. I set God deadlines that have more to do with my desperation and fear than with my faith in God's faithfulness. I think to myself, 'If the money I'm waiting for doesn't come in this morning's post, then I'll be in the red.' So I put all my 'faith' in the postman instead of in Jesus, and when the postman delivers only bills, I'm in despair. It's at that point the real test of faith begins; I may think I've already been tested, but until then I've only really been going through the storms of doubt, not the test of faith. I say, 'This morning's post, Lord,' and he says, 'No, the test of faith begins *after* this morning's post.' If I give up after the morning delivery I've failed the test and missed the answer that's coming in the afternoon. It's not that God is only the God of the second postal delivery, but I've never known him make a delivery too early! Watch out for these tests of faith, because your faithfulness and obedience in them are a direct route to pleasing the heart of your Father, and you'll learn lots about his character in them. What's more, in addition to hearing, seeing and doing, those very tests will build your faith.

Lastwords

I know the things in this book work for two reasons. Because
they're in God's book, and he doesn't lie, and because I'm
struggling towards the things I've written of with *his* power.
Take from here the things that are useful and let Jesus build
them into your spirit and your character. Thank you for the
opportunity of sharing these words with you, and remember
that at the end of the day it's not what you hear or read that
counts....

> Therefore, get rid of all moral filth and the evil that is so prevalent,
> and humbly accept the word planted in you, which can save you.
> Do not merely listen to the word, and so deceive yourselves. Do
> what it says. Anyone who listens to the word but does not do
> what it says is like a man who looks at his face in a mirror and,
> after looking at himself, goes away and immediately forgets what
> he looks like. But the man who looks intently into the perfect law
> that gives freedom, and continues to do this, not forgetting what
> he has heard, but doing it—he will be blessed in what he does
> (James 1:21–25).

It's what you *do* that counts for Jesus.

Addresses for Correspondence Courses

London Bible College
Green Lane
Northwood
Middx HA6 2UW
– ask for their foundation
courses.

Salvation Army
101 Queen Victoria Street
London EC4P 4EP
– label your letter 'For the
information of the
Education Department' if
you are under 18.

Salvation Army
International Training
College
Denmark Hill
London SE5
– label your correspondence
'To the Education Officer'
if you are 18 or over.

International
Correspondence Inst.
The Grove
London Road
Nantwich
Cheshire CW5 6LW
– ask either for basic or
intermediate courses; there
is a choice of 18 courses
under each heading.

The Occult And Young People

by Roger Ellis

Witches, horoscopes, ouija boards, reincarnation...

Day by day our senses are bombarded by occult propaganda; books on spiritism, newspaper reports on the paranormal, horoscopes on the radio, while New Age is all the rage.

This book warns of the dangers of dabbling with forces beyond our control. It also shows a way out for those who have been spiritually and emotionally wounded by demonic powers.

Roger Ellis lays the groundwork for a biblical understanding of the occult and the supernatural, as well as showing us how to take a positive Christian stand in spiritual warfare.

Roger Ellis is based at the Revelation Christian Fellowship in Sussex. He is a member of the Pioneer Team, and has been a regular speaker at Spring Harvest.

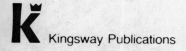

Kingsway Publications

Angels With Dirty Faces

by Ishmael

Ishmael loves children. Here's how—and why.

'Through all the years I've never known anyone who can so motivate children in worship, or lead them so securely into the things of the Spirit of God.'

—**Jim Graham, Pastor,
Goldhill Baptist Church.**

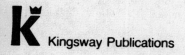
Kingsway Publications

The History of Ishmael

by Ian Smale

Ishmael—what do you make of him?

Don't think of an answer just now—suspend judgement for a while, and let him speak for himself.

Tongues before the 'charismatic movement'. Early rock 'n' roll at the Girl Guides. Life on the farm (it shouldn't happen to a choirboy). And the price of fame, the serious truth behind the humorous stage image.

It's all here, told as only Ishmael could tell it.

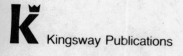

Kingsway Publications